THE
LITTLE
BOOK
OF
CAMBRIDGESHIRE

CAROLINE CLIFFORD
& ALAN AKEROYD

The
History
Press

First published 2018

The History Press
The Mill, Brimscombe Port
Stroud, Gloucestershire, GL5 2QG
www.thehistorypress.co.uk

British Library Cataloguing in Publication Data.
A catalogue record for this book is available from the British Library.

ISBN 978 0 7509 8555 0

Typesetting and origination by The History Press
Printed and bound in Great Britain by TJ International Ltd

CONTENTS

INTRODUCTION

Modern Cambridgeshire is in fact three counties: the historic county of Cambridgeshire, which is just the area around Cambridge; the Isle of Ely to its north; and Huntingdonshire to the west. From 1974 to 1998 the county also included the Peterborough area, which has switched between Northamptonshire, Huntingdonshire and Cambridgeshire from time to time and, although still part of the ceremonial county of Cambridgeshire, is now a unitary authority in its own right. Peterborough is the largest city in the ceremonial county.

The City of Cambridge is known mainly for its University, one of the most famous in the world. The University has had a huge impact on Cambridgeshire and has attracted many of the world's leading minds. But there is more to Cambridgeshire than the academics. The only commoner ever to be offered the British Crown was born here, along with many other leading figures, as we shall see in later chapters.

Cambridgeshire is the fifteenth largest county in England by area, covering 1,309 square miles (3,389 square kilometres) and is 27th out of 48 by population. The estimated population in 2016 (the latest figure available at the time of writing) was 849,035. It is one of the fastest growing areas in the country.

The former counties of the Isle of Ely and Huntingdonshire are the flattest districts in England. The highest point in the Isle is at Haddenham, just 39m above sea level. Huntingdonshire's highest point is 80m above sea level at Boring Field near Covington. The highest point in Cambridgeshire, at 146m above sea level, is near Great Chishill on the Essex border. Huntingdonshire also has the distinction of having the lowest point in the UK, Holme Fen, at almost 3m *below* sea level (and still sinking!). The Fens occupy the northern part of the modern county and are completely different from the rest of the county, as you will discover when you read this book.

Read on to find out more about this unique county – or counties.

1

50 THINGS YOU MAY NOT KNOW ABOUT CAMBRIDGESHIRE

1. The only person to have assassinated a British Prime Minister, John Bellingham, was born in St Neots (he shot Spencer Percival in the lobby of the Palace of Westminster in May 1812).
2. Diarist John Evelyn described Cambridge as a 'low, dirty and unpleasant place, the street ill paved, the air thick and infected by fens'.
3. The Prime Meridian runs through fifteen different parishes in Cambridgeshire and Huntingdonshire, from Coates in the north to Melbourn in the south.
4. The 44th President of the United States Barack Obama's grandmother is buried in Stapleford.
5. Marshall Aerospace in Cambridge built the droop nose for Concorde.
6. Parker's Piece in Cambridge is the birthplace of football.
7. There was a pet cemetery at Molesworth between 1909 and the 1950s. Over 800 burials of pets, mainly from London, took place there.
8. The chimes of Big Ben were copied from the original Cambridge chimes of the University Church of Great St Mary in 1793.

9. Cambridge did not become a city until 1951. It is one of only a few cities in the UK without a cathedral.
10. Barrington has the longest village green in England – half a mile long and covering 30 acres.
11. The first President of the United States George Washington's great-uncle Godfrey Washington was vicar of Little St Mary's in Cambridge. His coat of arms forms the basis of the stars and stripes flag.
12. The MG Owners Club has its UK headquarters at Swavesey.
13. The Cambridgeshire Guided Busway is the longest in the world.
14. The World Pea Shooting Championships have been held at Witcham since 1971. They were originally held to raise funds for the village hall.
15. There was a POW camp at Norman Cross for soldiers captured during the Napoleonic Wars. It was designed on principles that have since become standard across the world. By April 1810 there were 6,272 prisoners there. It was the second such prison; one had previously been set up in Gloucestershire for prisoners from the American War of Independence.
16. The area of market gardens near Christ's Pieces, Cambridge, was called the Garden of Eden – recognised now by street names Eden, Adam, Eve and Paradise streets. The whole area is known as 'the Kite' because of its shape.
17. Parker of Parker's Piece in Cambridge was a college cook who leased the land from Trinity College when it was exchanged by the college for land off Garret Hostel Lane which became part of the college.
18. Airman Homer, based with the 358th Bomber Squadron at Molesworth, was reportedly awarded the Air Medal for participating in five combat missions. Why was this unusual? He was a dog!
19. The Grafton Centre was named after Augustus Fitzroy, Duke of Grafton, Vice Chancellor of the University at the time when the area was first built on in the seventeenth century.
20. Portholme is the largest meadow in Europe, according to Arthur Mee in his King's England series. These days it is divided by the railway cutting through it. The fact that it

regularly floods makes it good for growing grass (a meadow is an area that is cut for hay).

21. The first car based in Cambridge is believed to have been a Peugeot Phaeton belonging to student Charles Rolls, who later went on to found the company Rolls-Royce with Henry Royce from Alwalton.

22. The first ever Village College, providing all sorts of education from the cradle to the grave, was set up at Sawston.

23. The discoveries at Must Farm near Whittlesey have been described as 'the Bronze Age Pompeii'.

24. During the First World War Huntingdonshire had a Cyclist Battalion.

25. The first set of quads to survive in Britain were born in St Neots. Ann, Ernest, Paul and Michael Miles (the St Neots Quads) were born in November 1935. They caused a sensation and people were charged a shilling to look at them in their nursery through the window of their council house in Eynesbury. Lucrative endorsements and sponsorship enabled the family to move from Eynesbury to St Neots. They made guest appearances at functions and were presented to the Duchess of Gloucester at Hinchingbrooke during the Second World War. Their latest appearance together was at St Neots Museum to celebrate their 80th birthdays in 2015.

26. Cambridge's famous Bumps Rowing races are held because the river is too narrow for proper racing.

27. The King Edward potato was developed and named by a Ramsey farmer, Jabez Papworth.

28. Oliver Cromwell's head is buried in Cambridge. Three years after Cromwell's death in 1658, Charles II ordered the dead body to be exhumed and then hanged, drawn and quartered. Cromwell's head was then skewered on a spike at Westminster. For several centuries the head travelled widely, being bought and sold by various entrepreneurs and showmen wishing to profit from displaying it. In 1841, Cromwell's head was bought by a Mr Josiah Wilkinson. In 1960, the Wilkinson family wished to arrange a proper burial, so contacted Sidney Sussex College in Cambridge, where Cromwell had once briefly studied. After some debate the college decided to bury the head in a secret

location. A plaque close to the burial site commemorates the curious interment on 25 March 1960 somewhere within the ante-chapel at the college. The precise spot was left unmarked. Cromwell's well-travelled head could finally rest in peace.

29. During the Second World War, Queen Marie of Yugoslavia lived in Great Gransden.

30. The term 'wooden spoon' is derived from the one that was awarded to the person with the lowest mark in the Cambridge University mathematics tripos. It was last awarded in 1909.

31. At one time, there were two shopkeepers in King's Parade Cambridge named Greef and Sadd. Mr Death lived nearby in King Street. H.E. Greef was a plumber, glazier and decorator as wells as captain of the voluntary fire brigade, Alfred Saad was a numismatist and antiquary, and John Death, who lived at Poplar House, was a Justice of the Peace. They all appear in the 1891 street directory.

32. Huntingdon's Thinking Soldier First World War Memorial was sculpted by Kathleen Scott, widow of Scott of the Antarctic.

33. Cambridge has a statue to a road sweeper in the Market Square. Snowy Farr used to carry live animals around on his cart and raised large amounts of money for the Guide Dogs for the Blind charity.

34. Chippenham was Britain's first Estate Village, set up by Edward Russell, Lord Orford (who also travelled around the Fens in a sailing boat).

35. Isiah Deck, a pharmaceutical chemist in Cambridge in the early 1800s, used to set off large rockets outside King's College each New Year's Eve. In 1838 he was put in charge of the fireworks committee for Queen Victoria's coronation feast.

36. China's most famous poet, Xu Zhimo, has a memorial in King's College inscribed with two verses of his poem 'A Second Farewell to Cambridge' (in Chinese).

37. An early electric lamp post on Parker's Piece in Cambridge has been named 'Reality Checkpoint' as it is thought to be the point where student Cambridge ends and real life begins.

38. Number 7A Jesus Lane in Cambridge (now Pizza Express) was once a Turkish Bath House.
39. The barrows at Bartlow Hills in Cambridgeshire are the largest surviving Roman burial mounds in Western Europe.
40. In the second half of the nineteenth century there was a lucrative industry in the Cambridgeshire fens, mainly around Burwell and Wicken, digging coprolite. Coprolite means 'dung stone' from the Greek. These fossilised remains were dug up and used as fertiliser. Most of what was found was actually dinosaur fossils rather than dung.
41. St Ives Bridge is one of only four in the country to incorporate a chapel. Between 1736 and 1930 it had two extra storeys.

42. Hilton village has one of only eight surviving ancient turf mazes in England. It was cut in 1660.
43. What is thought to be the oldest set of Christian church plate in the world was discovered at Water Newton.
44. In the early 1970s a hover train was tested on a specially built track between Earith and Sutton Gault.
45. Olaudah Equiano, a former slave kidnapped from Nigeria when he was 10 years old and later known as Gustavus Vassa, married Susanna Cullen from Soham in 1792.

46. The Gog Magog Hills are named after two giants from the Book of Revelations and got their name due to a large phallic figure once cut into the turf there.
47. In 1970 there was a student riot in Cambridge. The 'Garden House Riot' was against the fascist government in Greece and resulted in eight students being sentenced to imprisonment. The event was a turning point in student protests in Britain.
48. Queen Catherine of Aragon, first wife of Henry VIII, is buried in Peterborough Cathedral.
49. Holme Fen is the lowest point in Britain, 9ft below sea level.
50. More than 12,000 people sat down to dine on Parker's Piece to celebrate Queen Victoria's coronation in 1838.

2

THE UNIVERSITY OF CAMBRIDGE

Along with its great rival, Oxford, Cambridge is probably the most famous university in the world. The University recently celebrated its 800th anniversary (in 2009); it has dominated the town and later City of Cambridge for all that time. The University could merit several books on its own – we are recording here just a few items we think are of interest.

The University has around 18,000 full-time students (2016/17 figure), which is actually quite small compared with the more than 40,000 students at Manchester and 32,000 at Leeds. There are around 11,500 staff. 62 per cent of the students are undergraduates and 38 per cent postgraduate. The male/female ratio is 54 per cent male and 46 per cent female.

The University is made up of thirty-one individual colleges. Peterhouse is the oldest college, founded in 1284; Clare is the second oldest, founded in 1326. Seven colleges have been founded since 1950. The newest is Robinson College, founded in 1977, although Homerton College is the last institution to have achieved full college status (2010). Before that it was a teacher training college.

The most famous area of rivalry between the Universities of Cambridge and Oxford is the annual Boat Race, held on a 4-mile course between Putney and Mortlake on the River Thames. The first men's race was held in 1829 and it became an annual fixture in 1856. Cambridge has eighty-three wins in the men's race to Oxford's eighty. In 1927 the first women's race was held and this

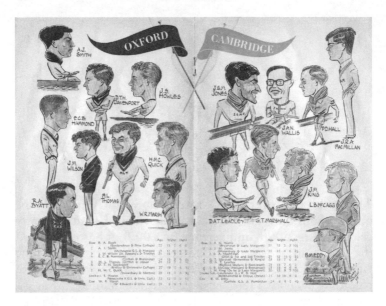

too became an annual event from 1964. Cambridge have won the women's race forty-three times to Oxford's thirty. Since 2015 the two races have been held on the same day.

To celebrate its 600th anniversary in 1884, Peterhouse College became the second place in England to use electricity (after the Houses of Parliament). Peterhouse is the smallest of the colleges.

Peterhouse has a history of multiple exorcisms. In 1997 ghost sightings at the college made national news. The apparition was identified as Francis Dawes, a former bursar, who had committed suicide in 1789 after the election of an unpopular master. An exorcism was said to have been carried out in 1999. Two previous exorcisms had already been carried out in the college. In the eighteenth century a poltergeist was removed from a student's room and a former dean carried out a ceremony because of the appearance of a dark presence in a corner of the old courtyard, overlooking the graveyard.

Corpus Christi College is the only college at either Oxford or Cambridge to be founded by the citizens of the town rather than by wealthy patrons.

Darwin College was built on land owned by the Darwin family. It accepts graduates only.

Trinity College, founded by Henry VIII, is the largest and wealthiest of the colleges. The statue of the king on the Great Gate was tampered with in the late 1800s: Henry's sceptre was removed from his hand and replaced with a chair leg.

King's College was founded by Henry VI in 1441 as a college to take students from his other foundation, Eton College. The foundation stone of the chapel was laid in 1446, but its construction was delayed by the Wars of the Roses and the chapel was finally ready for use in the reign of Henry VIII, nearly a century after it was begun. King's College Chapel receives around 230,000 visitors each year. Its Christmas service, the Festival of Nine Lessons and Carols, was first broadcast in 1928 and is now televised around the world.

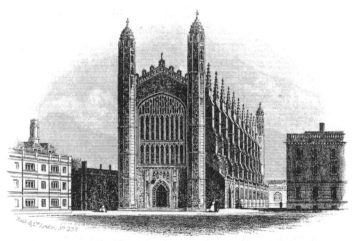

Chapel of King's College Cambridge.

The windows of King's College Chapel, unlike windows in other colleges, miraculously survived the destruction wrought by Puritan iconoclasts in the English Civil War. During the Second World War, however, the glass was removed from the windows and stored in cellars around Cambridge. They were replaced by grey tar-paper, with a few strips of plain glass at the bottom to let in some light.

The 'Cambridge Rules', drawn up in 1848, are the basis of the modern rules for football used by the English FA.

The youngest ever student was William Wooten, aged 9 (1675).

Three signatories of the American Declaration of Independence attended Cambridge University: Carolina Representatives Thomas Lynch Jr (Caius) and Arthur Middleton (Trinity Hall), and Virginia delegate Thomas Nelson Jr (Christ's).

The Queen Mother (Queen Elizabeth at the time) was the first woman to be awarded a degree in Senate House in 1948.

The infamous Soviet spies Donald Maclean (Trinity Hall), Guy Burgess, Kim Philby and Anthony Blunt (all Trinity) (the latter was only exposed as a spy in 1979), were known as 'the Cambridge Spies' because that is where they were recruited.

The Cambridge 'Footlights' Amateur Dramatic Club is where numerous famous performers including Emma Thompson, Hugh Laurie, Stephen Fry and David Mitchell started their careers. Performances are regularly staged at the ADC Theatre.

The debating chamber of the Cambridge Union was used by Field Marshall Montgomery to plan the D-Day landings in Normandy in the Second World War.

It is at Trinity College that the Great Court Run is attempted, a feat made famous in the 1981 film *Chariots of Fire*. In 1927 David Cecil, Lord Burghley, became the first and only person to officially run around the court whilst the college clock struck noon, a distance of 370m, in 43 seconds. He went on to win gold in the 400m hurdles at the 1928 Olympics in Amsterdam. The race was recreated for charity in 1988. Sebastian Coe and Steve Cram attempted the feat, but neither beat the clock (Coe won in 46 seconds). In 2007 a second-year economics undergraduate, Sam Dobin, completed the run as the chimes stopped, but ran on the cobbles rather than the path, which makes the run easier (and slightly shorter), so it didn't officially count.

In addition to the great University Library, one of the UK's five copyright libraries entitled to receive a copy of every book published in the country, Cambridge University has two other famous libraries. One is the Wren Library at Trinity College, which was designed by Sir Christopher Wren. Wren was the nephew of Bishop Matthew Wren of Ely. The Bishop had been imprisoned for eighteen years during the Civil War and when he was released he invited his nephew to design and build a new chapel at Pembroke College. This was Christopher's first major project. Five years later he designed a chapel for Emmanuel College, but of course he is much better known as the architect who designed St Paul's Cathedral in London.

Library Trinity College, Cambridge.

The University Library contains many treasures, including the first edition of Isaac Newton's *Principia Mathematica*, with handwritten notes for the second edition, and an eighth-century copy of the epistles of St Paul as well as first editions of Shelley, Wordsworth, Byron and Tennyson. Rare handwritten manuscripts and notebooks are also to be found in the collection, including the manuscript version of A.A. Milne's *Winnie the Pooh* and notes on the nuclear test programme by Robert Oppenheimer. Many of its treasures are now being digitised.

The other famous library is the Pepys Library at Magdalene College, bequeathed to his old college by the diarist Samuel Pepys. The library is made up of 3,000 volumes and attracts tourists and scholars from across the world.

The University has more than 100 libraries in total.

Cambridge University has the most Nobel laureates of any institution – ninety-eight since 1904 (at the time of writing). Affiliates of the University have won Nobel Prizes in every category: thirty-two in Physics, twenty-six in Medicine, twenty-four in Chemistry, eleven in Economics, three in Literature and two in Peace. Trinity alone has had thirty-two Nobel Prize winners. Frederick Sanger, from St John's and Fellow of King's, is one of only four individuals to have been awarded a Nobel Prize twice. He received the Nobel Prize in Chemistry in 1958 and 1980.

In 1857 graduates of the University petitioned the Cambridge University Commissioners to remove the condition of compulsory celibacy from the appointment to 'Fellow' of the University. Tenure of a Fellowship meant that marriage was out of the question.

The aim of the Cambridge night climbers is to leave their mark on the roofs of the college buildings. The earliest known night climber was Peter Gunning of Ely, who left an inscription on a lead slab on the roof of St John's in 1734. Lord Byron was reputedly the first to climb the Trinity Great Court fountain and scale the Wren Library. Night climbing became so popular at the end of the nineteenth century that *The Roof-Climbers' Guide to Trinity* was published in 1900 as a May Week joke. A guide to climbing St John's was published in 1921. In 1949 a bicycle was placed on a weathervane on the School of Geography in Downing Place. Many small objects have been placed on the spires of King's College Chapel, including four Santa hats on the four spires in 2009. It cost the college several thousand pounds to have them removed.

On 7 June 1958 engineering students from Gonville and Caius College hoisted an Austin 7 car onto the roof of the Senate House. It was a remarkable achievement and it took the authorities several days and a large crane to get it down again.

Magdalene College was the last all-male college in Oxford or Cambridge. Women were finally admitted in 1988. There are, however, still three all-female colleges: Lucy Cavendish (for mature students), Murray Edwards College and Newnham College. The first mixed college was Darwin, which was founded as a mixed college in 1964. Churchill, King's and Clare were the first all-male colleges to admit women, in 1972. The first all-female college to admit men was Hughes Hall, in 1973.

Queens' College doesn't have an apostrophe between the *n* and *s* in its name because it was founded by two queens, Margaret of Anjou, wife of Henry VI, and Elizabeth Woodville, wife of Edward IV; this was probably the only thing the two women agreed on as their husbands fought against one another in the Wars of the Roses.

Theodore Roosevelt, twice President of the USA, was awarded an honorary degree from Oxford and Cambridge Universities in 1910.

In 1890, Philippa Fawcett scored the highest mark in the Cambridge University maths exam, a subject widely considered to be only suitable for men. This raised some awkward questions as, at the time, Cambridge did not allow women to be awarded degrees. Her success attracted widespread newspaper coverage and helped to silence the popular belief that the female brain was illogical and, consequently, women should be denied the vote.

Cambridge University Press (CUP) is the oldest continuously functioning publishing house in the world. It was founded with a licence from Henry VIII in 1534. The printer, Thomas Thomas, had premises on what is now Senate House Lawn. The Press has printed many major works over the years, including John Milton's *Lycidas*, Isaac Newton's *Principia Mathematica* (1713 edition), Ernest Rutherford's *Radio-activity*, and Noam Chomsky's *Language and Mind*.

CUP is also the oldest Bible publisher in the world. The first Cambridge Bible, a 'Geneva Bible', was printed in 1591. The Press still prints the Church of England Authorised Bible and Book of Common Prayer.

Cambridge University bookshop, on the corner of Market Street and Trinity Street, has been a bookshop since at least 1581. This is the longest time a single business has occupied a shop in the world. It has been known as the Cambridge University Press bookshop for twenty-five years. The premises are said to be haunted by the ghosts of a White Lady or girl with long blonde hair, accompanied by the scent of violets, and a man in Victorian evening dress.

Cambridge 'May Week' is in June. May Week sees a series of balls and parties at the colleges and may originally have been held before the exams as a means of relaxation to improve performance – this was soon found to not be the case!

The head of Oliver Cromwell, Lord Protector, was rescued from a pike on the top of Westminster Hall and spent many years in private hands. In 1960 it was buried somewhere in Sidney Sussex College – it is said that no one knows exactly where. A plaque in the chapel records that it is there somewhere.

Cambridge University opened the first University Training School for primary-age children in 2015 as part of their North West Cambridge development (Eddington).

FAMOUS STUDENTS AND MEMBERS OF THE UNIVERSITY

There are obviously far too many to list them all, so here is just a selection.

SCIENCE AND MATHS

Isaac Newton (Trinity), mathematician and astronomer, who is considered one of the most influential scientists of all time. He discovered gravity, the laws of motion and calculus.

James Clerk Maxwell's (Trinity) research into electromagnetic radiation would lead to the development of television, mobile phones and infra-red telescopes. The largest astronomical telescope in the world in Hawaii is named after him. He was also involved in the setting up of the Cavendish Laboratory and became the first Cavendish Professor of Physics. Others who worked at the Cavendish include **Joseph John Thompson**

STATUE OF SIR ISAAC NEWTON.
IN THE ANTE-CHAPEL, TRINITY COLLEGE.

(Trinity), the physicist who discovered the electron and the first sub-atomic particle, and his student **Ernest Rutherford** (also Trinity), known as the father of nuclear physics and chemistry.

Francis Crick (Gonville and Caius), **James Watson** (Clare) and **Rosalind Franklin** (Newnham) discovered the structure of DNA.

Stephen Hawking (Gonville and Caius) was the former Lucasian Professor of Mathematics at the University of Cambridge, author of *The Brief History of Time* and subject of the film *The Theory of Everything*.

Charles Babbage (Peterhouse) mathematician, codebreaker and pioneer of computing.

Alan Turing (King's), the Bletchley Park codebreaker. Other codebreakers associated with Cambridge are **Dilly Cox** (King's), **John Jeffreys** (Downing), **Gordon Welchman** (Fellow of Sidney Sussex) and **Max Newman** of St John's. Other inventors include **Frank Whittle** (Peterhouse), the inventor of the jet engine, and **Christopher Cockerell** (Peterhouse), who developed the hovercraft.

The field of natural history includes the man who proposed the theory of evolution by natural selection, **Charles Darwin** (Christ's), American zoologist **Dian Fossey** (Churchill), best known for her work with gorillas in Rwanda, and TV presenter and naturalist **David Attenborough** (Clare).

World-famous economist **John Maynard Keynes** (King's) was born and studied in Cambridge. The philosopher, statesman and scientist **Francis Bacon** went to Trinity College at the age of 12. It was there that he first met Queen Elizabeth I.

POETS AND WRITERS

The vast array of authors who have studied at Cambridge include **Sylvia Plath** (Newnham), **John Milton** (Christ's), **Christopher Marlowe** (Corpus Christi), **Rupert Brooke** (King's), **Siegfried Sassoon** (Clare), **Ted Hughes** (Pembroke), **Andrew Marvell** (Trinity), **Lord Byron** (Trinity), **Samuel Taylor Coleridge** (Jesus), **John Dryden** (Trinity), **Allama Muhammad Iqbal** (Trinity), **Alfred, Lord Tennyson** (Trinity), **A.A. Milne** (Trinity), **Salman Rushdie** (King's), **C.S. Lewis** (Magdalene), **Douglas Adams** (St John's), **Zadie Smith** (King's), **J.B. Priestley** (Trinity Hall) and **Germaine Greer** (Murray Edwards). The illustrator **Quentin Blake** studied at Downing College.

ACTORS AND TV STARS

Actors who studied at Cambridge include **Sir Ian McKellan** (St Catharine's), **Hugh Bonneville** (Corpus Christi), **Dan Stevens** (Emmanuel), **Tom Hiddleston** (Pembroke), **Derek Jacobi** (St John's), **Tom Hollander** (Selwyn), **Eddie Redmayne** (Trinity) and **James Norton** (Magdalene), **Emma Thompson** (Newnham), **Cherie Lunghi** (Homerton), **Tilda Swinton** (Murray Edwards) and **Rachel Weisz** (Trinity Hall). Film producer **Sam Mendes** studied at Peterhouse and director, scriptwriter and playwright **Stephen Poliakoff** studied at King's.

Comedians/actors/presenters include **Stephen Fry** (Queens') and **Hugh Laurie** (Selwyn), **John Cleese** (Downing) and fellow Monty Python members **Eric Idle** and **Graham Chapman**. The 'Goodies' all studied at Cambridge: **Tim Brooke Taylor, Bill Oddie** (both Pembroke) and **Graeme Garden** (Emmanuel). Others include **Sandi Toksvig** (Girton and Homerton), **Griff Rhys Jones** (Emmanuel), **Jimmy Carr** (Gonville and Caius), **David Baddiel** (King's), **David Mitchell** (Peterhouse), **Ben Miller** (St Catharine's), and **Hugh Dennis** (St John's).

Sacha Baron Cohen, the creator of Ali G and Borat, studied at Christ's and his cousin **Simon Baron Cohen** is a Fellow of Trinity College, Professor of Developmental Psychopathology and Directory of the University's Autism Research Centre.

Other TV favourites from Cambridge include **Sue Perkins** (Murray Edwards) and **Mel Giedroyc** (Trinity), comedians who became stars of the BBC's *The Great British Bake-Off*, **Clive Anderson** (Selwyn), *Blue Peter* presenter **Konnie Huq** (Robinson), *Countdown* maths expert **Carol Vorderman** (Sidney Sussex), historian **Simon Schama** (Christ's), former *Newsnight* presenter who now presents the quiz show *University Challenge* **Jeremy Paxman** (St Catharine's), TV host **David Frost** (Gonville and Caius), **Loyd Grossman** (Magdalene), radio presenter **Vanessa Feltz** (Trinity), news reporter **John Simpson** (Magdalene) and political presenter **Andrew Marr** (Trinity Hall).

POLITICS

British politicians who studied at Cambridge include our first Prime Minister **Robert Walpole** (King's) and **William Pitt the Younger** (Pembroke), our youngest ever Prime Minister at 24. Other Cambridge alumni who led the country are **Viscount Palmerston** (St John's), **Arthur Balfour, Stanley Baldwin, Henry Campbell Bannerman, Viscount Melbourne** and **Earl Grey**, all of Trinity College. **William Wilberforce** (St John's), the anti-slavery campaigner, became a lifelong friend of William Pitt at Cambridge.

More recent political figures include **Nick Clegg** (Robinson), **Diane Abbott** (Newnham), **Vince Cable** (Fitzwilliam), **David Owen** (Sidney Sussex), **Michael Portillo** (Peterhouse), **Andy Burnham** (Fitzwilliam) and **Alistair Campbell** (Gonville and Caius).

Many foreign leaders have also studied at Cambridge, including the first Prime Minister of an independent India, **Jawaharlal Nehru** (Trinity) and his grandson, also Prime Minister of India, **Rajiv Ghandi** (Trinity), who was assassinated in 1991. **Stanley**

Bruce (Trinity Hall), Prime Minister of Australia 1923–29, and **Jan Smuts** (Christ's), Prime Minister of South Africa, studied in Cambridge between 1919–24 and 1939–48.

SPORT

Sporting alumni include England cricket captains **Mike Atherton** (Downing), **Ted Dexter** (King's), and **Mike Brierley** (St John's). Rugby internationals and Captains of the British and Irish Lions **Gavin Hastings** (Magdalene) and **Rob Andrew** (St John's). Athletes **David Cecil, Lord Burghley** (Magdalene), **Chris Brasher** (St John's) and **Harold Abrahams** (Gonville and Caius), Olympic gold medallist in modern pentathlon **Stephanie Cook** (Peterhouse) and triathletes **Alistair Brownlee** (Girton) and **Emma Pooley** (Trinity Hall), who also won an Olympic silver medal for cycling. The legendary darts commentator **Sid Waddell** studied at St John's.

THE OLD BRIDGE, S. JOHN'S COLLEGE.

A few other famous alumni include Archbishops **Michael Ramsey** (Magdalene), **Rowan Williams** (Clare), **Justin Welby** (Trinity) and **John Sentamu** (Selwyn); the envoy held hostage for five years in Beirut, **Terry Waite** (Trinity Hall); the *Downton Abbey* creator **Julian Fellowes** (Magdalene); and former Governor of the Bank of England **Mervyn King** (St John's).

Others include the mountaineer who died on the ascent – or was it the descent? – of Everest, **George Mallory** (Magdalene), **John Harvard,** founder of Harvard University (Emmanuel) and **Prince Charles** (Trinity).

3

SAINTS AND SINNERS

SAINTS

There are thousands of saints associated with the early Christian church and many continue to be added to the list. Cambridgeshire had several important religious institutions (see Chapter 9), but these don't appear to have produced many celebrated holy figures. There are, however, several saints at least loosely associated with the county.

The creation of saints in the early Christian church was a rather informal affair. Popular acclaim could confer sainthood without the necessity for official confirmation from the Vatican. The medieval obsession with relics, which were believed to have miraculous properties of healing and forgiveness, meant that the possession of a whole body of a saint would be a wonderful thing for a church or abbey. Newly established abbeys like Ramsey needed something to attract pilgrims.

So it was that when some ancient bones along with some religious tokens were unearthed at Slepe, an area under the control of Ramsey Abbey in around 1001 or 1002, the stage was set for a miraculous occurrence. The only information about the bones came to a local blacksmith in a dream. The body identified itself as Ivo, a Persian bishop who had come to England. The vision also appeared to the local bailiff and, when a stone coffin was also discovered, it was obvious that he was a saint. The body was transferred to Ramsey Abbey and became **St Ivo**. The village of Slepe soon became known as St Ives.

St Neot is thought to have been a brother of King Alfred named Athelstan, who took holy orders and changed his name. 'Neot' means 'little one' and it is likely that he was of very short stature. He is sometimes referred to as 'the pigmy saint', but this could be due to confusion over the size of the box his bones were kept in rather than his actual size. St Neot was buried in Cornwall.

Over 230 miles away in Huntingdonshire a shrine had been built to Ernulf at Eynesbury. For some reason (bribery, perhaps, or instruction from on high) the warden of the shrine in Cornwall agreed to move the bones of Neot to Eynesbury. A raiding party accompanied the bones and drove off the enraged Cornishmen. The nearby town became known as St Neots in the saint's honour.

St Neot is not the only saint who was buried in Cambridgeshire after some rather underhand practices.

St Withburga (or Wihtburh) was a princess and later abbess who founded a convent at Dereham. When she had nothing to feed the workman building the convent, a vision of the Virgin Mary directed her to two does that appeared and provided milk for them. Withburga died in 743 and was buried at Ely Abbey. When her body was dug up fifty-five years later it was found not to have decayed. This was considered a miracle and she was reburied as a saint in a church she had founded in Dereham, Norfolk. This church became a place of pilgrimage.

In 974, Brithnoth, Abbot of Ely, decided that his abbey could profit from having a saint, so he decided to steal the body. He went to Dereham with several armed men and invited the Dereham men to a feast. Whilst they were drunk, Brithnoth and his men made off with the body. When the Dereham men discovered what had happened they gave chase, but despite a fight could not follow through the marshes round Ely. St Withburga was buried in Ely. However, a spring had arisen in the violated tomb at Dereham and pilgrims continued to visit. The spring has never run dry.

St Withburga is associated with a Cambridgeshire oddity – the Floating Church of St Withburga of Holme. Holme was an isolated rural parish and many parts were inaccessible and cut off from the church. There were, however, 9 miles of navigable waterway in the parish, so when the Rev. George Broke became vicar in 1895 he thought he would make use of them. He decided to use a boat as a church. One idea was to strap a disused railway carriage onto a barge, but in the end a houseboat was built, 30ft long and 9ft wide. It housed a small altar, a miniature font and a small American organ. Nearly fifty people could sit in the church. The church was used between 1899 and 1907. It was subsequently bought by some local men and renamed 'Saints Rest' but it finally sank in 1912.

Nothing much is known about **St Pandionia,** who is also known as Pandonia or Pandwina. She was born in Scotland or Ireland and died in around AD 904. Leland, the hagiographer, claimed she was the daughter of a Scottish king who fled from those who would deflower her. She took refuge with a kinswoman, who was prioress at Eltisley. She may have been a virgin martyr. She was buried in the church that bears her name in Eltisley. Her saint's day is 26 August.

St Etheldreda, also known as Audrey, was born at Exning, the daughter of King Anna and sister of Withburga. She left her second husband and founded the monastery at Ely in AD 673.

She died from the plague in AD 680. Seventeen years later her body was exhumed and found to be intact – this was deemed a miracle and she became a saint. The body was reburied in a Roman sarcophagus. Her shroud and coffin were said to have the power to cure infirmities, but that didn't stop her shrine at Ely from being destroyed in 1541. The relics were lost, apart from her left hand, which reappeared in 1810!

The fair held in the Middle Ages on her feast day was notorious for selling low-quality cheap necklaces of silk and lace, which were described as 'of St Audrey'. This was later shortened to the word 'tawdry', meaning goods of poor or inferior quality.

St Wendreda was also related to the royal house of Anna, a family which played a large part in the expansion of Christianity in East Anglia. She spent her life doing good works and practising herbal medicine. Later in life she had a calling to move to March, a damp and dismal place in the Fens, where she continued to treat the sick. Her body was buried at March where it was visited by pilgrims. The remains were later transferred to Ely, where they were enclosed in a shrine of gold, adorned with precious stones.

Wendreda's body was carried into battle by the Anglo–Saxon army of Edmund Ironside to bring them good fortune. It didn't work and they were defeated. The body was seized by King Cnut. On learning of the story of Wendreda, he was miraculously converted to Christianity and presented the body to Canterbury. Wendreda was finally returned to March in 1342.

St Pega came from a noble family of the ancient kingdom of Mercia but lived as a religious recluse near her brother Guthlac's hermitage at Crowland (he also became a saint). On her way to his funeral Pega was said to have cured a blind man from Wisbech. Pega went on a pilgrimage to Rome and died there in AD 719. It was claimed that her relics survived and performed miracles. It was said that her heart was returned to her home in the Fens, which was named 'Pega's Church' (Peakirk) in her honour.

SINNERS

Cambridgeshire, in common with most places, has produced far more sinners than saints.

The Burwell Fire. One of Cambridgeshire's worst crimes was at first thought to be an accident. In 1727, more than 100 spectators gathered in a barn in Burwell to watch a play put on by a travelling company led by Robert Shepheard. For some reason, possibly to stop more people sneaking in, the doors of the barn were nailed shut. An ostler, Richard Whittaker, tried to climb in through the loft and managed to set fire to some straw.

The fire swept through the barn and no one could escape. Panic broke out and some people were trampled. Others perished in the fire before rescuers could break in. Seventy-six people died that day and two more succumbed to their wounds later. Richard Whittaker claimed his innocence and was cleared of arson at the Cambridge Assizes. That would have been the end of the matter had it not been for a report in the *Cambridge Chronicle* on 19 February 1774 that claimed a man (unnamed) had confessed to starting the fire. The general belief was that it was Richard Whittaker, who had a grudge against Shepheard.

In 2005 a memorial was placed at the site of the barn, in what is now called Cuckold's Row.

Bring up the Bodies. One of the more bizarre cases from Cambridgeshire history is that of the Yaxley body-snatchers.

Until 1832, doctors, medical schools and hospitals were legally only allowed to carry out medical research on the bodies of recently executed criminals. As there were not nearly enough of these to meet demand, some anatomists paid body-snatchers (or 'Resurrectionists' as they were also known) to raid new graves and supply them with corpses.

Rumours about body-snatching around Peterborough began to spread in late 1830 when the body of a recently buried woman from Yaxley was found hidden in a brewhouse. This led to the discovery that bodies had been removed from several churchyards in the area. Two men from Farcet were eventually apprehended and tried at the Huntingdonshire

Quarter Sessions. Evidence from the trial is held at the Huntingdonshire Archives.

William Patrick and his accomplice William Whayley were charged with stealing a body. Both men admitted the offence and said that the bodies they had removed were passed to a Mr Grimmer, who took them to London. Whayley provided evidence against Patrick and was released without charge. Patrick was found guilty and sentenced to twelve months' imprisonment in the County Gaol. As far as we know, the mysterious Mr Grimmer was never found. A newspaper report at the time reveals that the judge wanted to add 'hard labour' to the term, but the law did not allow it (the law at this time was much more concerned with crimes against property than against the person. Assaults, even if someone was killed, were often treated more leniently than theft).

The story of the Yaxley body-snatchers is further complicated by a case of mistaken identity. The stolen body of Jane Mason, from Yaxley, was mistaken for that of Elizabeth Billings, a young woman whose body had been taken from Cowgate cemetery in Peterborough. Jane's body was put into Elizabeth's grave until the mistake was realised. It was only then that Jane was identified and returned to Yaxley for a third and final burial.

The body-snatching at Yaxley wasn't an isolated incident. There were reports of attempts to steal bodies at Cherry Hinton and Barnwell in 1827 and 1828. It appeared that the main market for bodies was London and the business of supplying bodies appeared to be an early form of mail order. In 1831 a suspicious hamper was opened at the mail office in Cambridge. It was found to contain the body of a young woman who had died and had been buried in Ely. The hamper was addressed to a London surgeon. A similar hamper was delivered to the Horse and Gate pub in Chatteris, destined for the Wisbech to London coach. The string that fastened the hamper broke; it came open and was found to contain the bodies of a woman and two infants.

The alternative was equally as bad. There was a widespread belief that the authorities were selling paupers' bodies to Addenbrooke's Hospital. People in Cambridge attacked the Anatomy School after it was reported that the body of a

pauper had been sent there for dissection. A riot ensued and the premises were broken into. Specimen cases were smashed and the building ransacked, but nothing was found.

J.H. Leech, the University Chemist, advertised the sale of complete skeletons, skulls and 'the Students' half set of bones' as well as dissection implements, so the fears of the locals were not entirely unfounded.

Dissection was not the only fate for executed prisoners. In the Chemical Lecture Room at the Botanical Garden in Cambridge, Professor Cumming conducted experiments with a powerful electric battery. Inspired no doubt by the sensational novel *Frankenstein* published in 1818, he attempted to 'galvanise' the body of the unfortunate criminal who had been executed just an hour before. The electric current caused the muscles of the arm and face to twitch and move. Presumably they were hoping to reanimate the body!

Death of the Prime Minister. Only one British Prime Minister has ever been assassinated. On 11 May 1812 Spencer Percival was shot through the heart in the lobby of the House of Commons. Huntingdonshire has the distinction of being the birthplace of the assassin.

John Bellingham was born in St Neots in 1776. He ran his own business but was arrested in Russia on suspicion of fraud. Although the charges were later dropped, by this time he had been made bankrupt. The British Embassy had refused to help Bellingham and he spent six years in prison. Understandably disillusioned and bitter, he wrote to the Prime Minister and petitioned Parliament for compensation. No one was willing to help him, so he went to Parliament armed with two pistols. When Percival entered the lobby, Bellingham calmly walked up and shot him in the chest. The Prime Minister was not popular and when news of the crime spread, a mob tried to free Bellingham from the coach that was transporting him to Newgate Gaol. They failed and he was quickly tried, found guilty and executed on 18 May. Spencer Percival left a widow and twelve children.

Later in the century another native of Huntingdonshire would prevent an assassination. In June 1867, a would-be assassin fired a pistol at both Tsar Alexander II of Russia and the French Emperor Napoleon III while in Paris. The attempt was thwarted by an aide-de-camp riding his horse between the gunman and the two emperors. The bullet hit the horse, which was killed, but the emperors were unharmed. The horse was named Cardigan and had been bred at Wansford near Peterborough by the landlord of the Haycock Inn. After several more attempts, Alexander II was finally killed by another assassin in 1881.

Martha Ray shot dead. Martha Ray was the long-time mistress of the Earl of Sandwich, with whom she had five surviving children. She was a talented singer and she and the Earl were wont to host glamorous musical parties at Hinchingbrooke House in Huntingdon. Martha had a brief affair with an ex-soldier, James Hackman, who became besotted with her, but she rejected him. In a fit of jealousy, he shot her dead on the steps of the Royal Opera House in Covent Garden. He turned the gun on himself, but only succeeded in grazing his head with the bullet. He was tried for murder and hanged on 19 April 1779.

The St Neots Poisoner. The case of Walter Horsford, the St Neots Poisoner, made headlines across the country as far afield as Aberdeen, Belfast and Truro. Walter, a farmer from Spaldwick near Huntingdon, was condemned and executed for poisoning his widowed cousin Annie Holmes with strychnine. Horsford had a brief affair with Annie and she became pregnant. Walter had recently married and, rather than cause a scandal, he agreed to try and help Annie get rid of the child. He sent her a powder to take with a note saying 'take a little in water, it is quite harmless'. The powder was strychnine and Annie died. The note from Horsford and the paper the poison was wrapped in were discovered in Annie's bedroom. A chemist testified that Horsford had purchased the poison from his shop. In June 1898 he was found guilty of murder and transferred to Cambridge gaol for execution. A special execution shed was built in the grounds of the gaol as executions were no longer carried out in public. When he heard the sound of hammering outside, Horsford was told that they were building an extension to the gaol.

Another noteworthy poisoning case saw the execution of **Mary Reeder**, aged 20, and **Elias Lucas**, aged 25, for the poisoning of Susan Lucas at Castle Camps. Susan was the sister of Mary Reeder, who had been having an affair with her brother-in-law. The pair gave the unfortunate Susan arsenic, but the doctor was suspicious of the suddenness and speed of her death. Mary and Elias were hanged together on 13 April 1850, the last public double execution in Cambridge. A crowd of 40,000 spectators gathered to watch. It was the custom to erect temporary stands around the gallows, which were situated at the old Cambridge Castle.

Paying the Ultimate Price. Between 1764 and 1804, sixty-six people were found guilty of capital crimes and sentenced to death at the Huntingdon Assizes and seventy-eight at the Cambridge Assizes. In the late 1700s this was not difficult as more than 200 different crimes carried the death penalty, including stealing a sheep or a horse.

Until 1836 a death sentence for murder was to be carried out two days after the sentence (unless that was a Sunday). After the hanging, the body was to be handed over to a surgeon for dissection or hung in chains at some suitable place – usually near the site of the murder. There is no record of any convicts from Cambridgeshire being hanged in chains, although this did happen once in Huntingdonshire and the Isle of Ely.

For crimes other than murder, executions were usually on a market day for maximum impact and deterrent.

Capital crimes included arson. Thomas Savage from Somersham was the last man executed for this crime in Cambridgeshire in 1824. His two accomplices secured their own pardons by turning King's evidence and accusing Savage of setting fire to a barn. The blaze had raged for three hours and damaged at least twenty properties.

The Littleport Riots of 1816 saw five men executed. Against the background of impoverishment across the country following the Napoleonic Wars there were disturbances across Norfolk and Suffolk. On 22 May a group of labourers gathered at the Globe public house in Littleport. The main topic of conversation was the disturbances elsewhere. At some point, they decided to join in and a stone was thrown through a shop window.

The vicar tried to get them to disperse and attempted to read the Riot Act – they told him to go home and later ransacked his house. The mob broke into several properties and smashed up furniture. Some householders gave them money to go away. Soldiers were sent for from Bury St Edmunds. The government was genuinely worried by the danger of violent protest getting out of hand; the revolution in France was still fresh in everyone's mind and any challenge to the establishment was seen to contain the seeds of revolution.

In the meantime, the rioters, numbering around 200 by this time, headed for Ely, some armed with fowling guns, pitchforks and other weapons. The local magistrate appealed to them to go home and some did. The others carried on attacking shops and were joined by some unruly Ely men. They extorted money from tradesmen and took beer from the pubs. They left Ely shortly before the soldiers arrived and returned to Littleport. The soldiers followed and found them in the George and Dragon public house. The rioters came out and attacked the soldiers but they were soon overpowered. One soldier was shot in the arm (he later lost it). He expressed his sadness that he had come through the Peninsula War and Battle of Waterloo unscathed only to be wounded by one of his own countrymen. Thomas Sindall, who tried to take a pistol from one of the soldiers, was shot dead as he ran off.

In total eighty-two people were arrested and taken to Ely. Articles valued at around £400 (more than £25,000 in today's money) were recovered. They appeared before Judge Edward Christian (who incidentally was the bother of Fletcher Christian of Mutiny on the *Bounty* fame). Twenty-three men and one woman were finally convicted, and they were all sentenced to death. Of these only five were actually executed, on Friday 28 June. One was transported for fourteen years, three for seven years and five for life. Ten were imprisoned for twelve months for stealing.

Those who were executed – William Beamiss, George Crow, John Dennis, Isaac Harley and Thomas South – were buried together at St Mary's Church in Ely, where a stone slab bears the inscription 'May their awful fate be a warning to others'. Only six other people were executed in Ely between 1800 and 1834.

As can be seen by the Littleport case, the Assize court judges would usually reprieve those condemned to death. Of the sixty-six people condemned in Huntingdonshire, only twelve were actually hanged and twenty-five from the seventy-eight condemned at Cambridge.

In 1864 **John Green** was the last person to be publicly hanged in Cambridgeshire. After that, the executions took place in a wooden shed in the grounds of the prison on Castle Hill.

John murdered Elizabeth Brown in Whittlesey when they were drunk on stolen gin. She refused his advances and he strangled and beat her, then tried to burn the body in a kiln in the Maltings where he worked. She may not have been dead before he set the body alight with burning sacks. He was executed on 2 January 1864. The judge described the case as 'one of the foulest murders that had ever disgraced the face of this earth'.

The last person to be publicly executed in Huntingdonshire was much earlier, in April 1829. **John Bishop** was found guilty of stealing twenty sheep from John and Thomas Lindsell of Hemingford Grey. He was condemned with 'no hopes of mercy on this side of the grave'. This was due not only to the magnitude of the crime, but also to the fact that he did not seem 'activated by want'. This verdict shows that the judges were not unaware of the financial hardships that drove some to crime.

The last execution in Wisbech was in 1819, one of only three since 1800.

CAMBRIDGE CASTLE.

Frederick Seekings was the last man to be executed in Cambridgeshire, in November 1913. He and his common-law wife argued and he cut her throat in the street when drunk after leaving the Bell Inn in Brampton.

The last Cambridgeshire man to be executed, on 10 July 1935, was **Walter Worthington** for the murder of his wife Sybil in Broughton. He became obsessively jealous and suspected his wife of betraying him with her nephew Lionel. He was executed outside the county at Bedford Gaol.

Transportation was often a preferred alternative to execution. Initially this was to America, but this had to stop after the War of Independence. Australia became a penal colony in 1788 and remained so until 1868. This was the fate of men like Andrew Stevens, who was sentenced to ten years' transportation at the Huntingdonshire Assizes for breaking into a house and stealing two coats, two pairs of trousers, one waistcoat, one cotton handkerchief, two gowns, one petticoat and one shawl. The records show that he was taken from Huntingdon gaol to Millbank in London, on the site of what is now Tate Britain, a holding prison for those about to be transported. He was then sent to the prison hulk *Justitia*, moored at Woolwich. About eighteen months after his conviction he was finally sent to Australia aboard the convict ship *Mermaid*. He arrived at the Swan River Colony, which had asked for prisoners to help build the infrastructure of the area, five months later. The colony later became Perth in Western Australia. Transported prisoners were not given a passage back to England.

SPIES IN CAMBRIDGESHIRE

As time went on, fewer crimes carried the death penalty. One that did, however, was treason. Cambridge is famous for its spies – Guy Burgess, Donald Maclean, Anthony Blunt (more about them later) – but they were not the first spies associated with the county.

In September 1940 Tom Cousins, a Private in the Home Guard, came across two men behaving rather suspiciously in a field near Willingham. He raised the alarm and the two were arrested by guards from nearby RAF Oakington. One of the men took his own life in custody, but the other, **Wulf Schmidt**, was interrogated. He was Danish by birth and had been recruited by the Nazis as a spy. Although he had second thoughts, he was sent to England, parachuted in with a radio and some English money. Given the choice between execution and working for Britain, he chose the latter and began sending messages drawn up by British Intelligence to his German masters. He was never suspected of being a double agent and was awarded the Iron Cross. After the war, he remained in Britain under the name Harold Williamson and died in London in 1992.

Josef Jakobs was not so lucky. He too was captured by a member of the Home Guard, Corporal H. Godfrey, near Ramsey. Like Schmidt he had been parachuted in equipped with a radio, £497 (in pound notes), some German sausage and a flask of brandy, and was carrying British identity papers. Unfortunately for him, he injured his ankle on landing. On examination his clothes were found to have German labels and his documents were written in continental script. He was taken to the Tower of London, where he was tried and executed in August 1941. His injured ankle meant that he was strapped to a chair to be shot. Josef Jakobs was the last person to be executed at the Tower. The chair remained on display there for some years.

Another German agent, a Dutch national, **Willem ter Braak** (real name Engelbertus Fukken) is buried in Great Shelford. He operated in England for five months in 1941 but when he ran out of money he committed suicide in a public air-raid shelter in Christ's Pieces in Cambridge. It was only in 2017 that the Parish Council agreed that a memorial stone could be erected in the village cemetery.

Some of the most prolific killers associated with Cambridge are the men known as **the Cambridge Spies**. By betraying those agents working for Britain, Kim Philby and his associates were responsible for the deaths of many. Largely recruited in Cambridge in the 1930s against a backdrop of peace protests and hunger marches, these spies remained undetected for many years. Guy Burgess (codename Hicks) worked for MI6, Donald Maclean (codename Homer) became a Foreign Office secretary. Kim Philby (codename Stanley) also worked for MI6 and as a journalist in Washington. They were members of a secret society known as 'the Apostles', an elitist, Marxist group based at King's and Trinity Colleges. Burgess and Maclean escaped to Moscow in 1951, just prior to being exposed. Philby followed in 1963.

Anthony Blunt (codename Johnson) was only revealed as the fourth man in 1979. He had been an MI5 officer and rose to become Director of the Courtauld Institute and Surveyor of the Queen's Pictures. He did a deal with the security services and escaped punishment until Margaret Thatcher found out and had him stripped of his knighthood and Fellowship of Trinity College.

The fifth man was probably John Cairncross, and art critic Brian Sewell may have been a sixth.

In 2002 Soham in Cambridgeshire became the focus of media attention during the investigation of one of the most notorious crimes in recent years. The cold-blooded murder of schoolgirls Holly Wells and Jessica Chapman by the school caretaker Ian Huntley, which his partner and their former teacher, Maxine Carr, helped him to cover up, shocked the whole nation. Things like this are mercifully rare in Cambridgeshire.

FIGHTING CRIME

Following the success of the Metropolitan Police, boroughs in the nineteenth century were instructed to set up a Watch Committee to appoint constables to police the towns. Trained men were sent out to help with this. The man sent to Cambridge stayed on as Superintendent of Police when the Borough Force was set up in 1836.

The County Police Act of 1839 permitted Justices of the Peace to set up a paid police force in their county. It was not compulsory and fewer than half of the English counties did so.

The Isle of Ely was one of the first, setting up a force in 1841. Cambridgeshire followed ten years later and Huntingdonshire only when setting up a police force became compulsory in 1857.

Setting up the Cambridgeshire force met with considerable opposition from ratepayers, who thought it would be too expensive. The total cost was estimated at £4,790 per year.

The Cambridgeshire and Huntingdonshire forces shared a Chief Constable, Captain George Davis RN. The Isle of Ely had their own Chief Constable, Captain Frederick Blogg Hampton, who was appointed when their force was set up in 1841.

The Cambridgeshire Constabulary was split into seven divisions: Arrington, Bottisham, Cambridge (excluding the Borough), Caxton, Cottenham, Linton and Newmarket. Each had a superintendent and a sergeant. With fifty-five constables, this made a total establishment of seventy men.

The Huntingdonshire Constabulary had a strength of forty men, including four superintendents, one inspector, three sergeants and thirty-two constables. Each superintendent was responsible for maintaining a horse and cart at his own expense.

There are now more than 1,300 officers in the Cambridgeshire Constabulary, which has a predicted gross revenue expenditure for 2018/19 approaching £140 million.

To start with, there were no police stations or lock-ups in Cambridgeshire. Superintendent Marsen had to keep prisoners under guard in his stable.

In 1912 plain clothes police were used to catch juveniles spinning tops in the street. Marbles were also to be confiscated. These undercover operators were known as 'Strange Officers'.

The first policewoman in Huntingdonshire, Eileen Lenton, was appointed in March 1946, shortly followed by the first police dog, Sabre, in 1952. Unfortunately, he had difficulty distinguishing between friends and foe and tended to bite everyone!

There were five police forces in the county – Cambridge Borough, Cambridge County, Peterborough Combined, Isle of Ely and Huntingdonshire. The forces were combined to form the Mid-Anglia Constabulary in 1965.

4

THE CAMBRIDGESHIRE FENS

The Fens extend across much of eastern England, from Lincolnshire in the north to Cambridgeshire in the south and today form one of Britain's richest agricultural areas. But it was not always so. Before the seventeenth century the Fens were largely a vast marshland wilderness that provided summer grazing for livestock and vast supplies of peat, fish and wildfowl. Roads were poor but irrelevant, because inhabitants largely travelled around the area by boat, using the many meandering and slow-moving waterways.

The land is exceptionally low-lying and for most of human history the Fens flooded completely during winter. Although fenland itself covers about 1,300 square miles it actually drains a much larger catchment area of almost 6,000 square miles, or most of central England. Before the fenland was drained in the seventeenth century, the Great Ouse River and its tributaries often burst their banks because they were not large enough to cope with the volume of water surging through them. The water could not easily soak into the ground because the underlying ground is solid clay, so every winter the water would lie on top of the ground until the natural rivers could carry it to the sea, which often took months.

Daniel Defoe saw one winter:

[the] Fen Country almost all covered with water like a sea: the Michaelmas Rains having been very great that year, they had sent floods of Water from the Upland Counties, and these fens being as may very properly be said the sink of no less that thirteen Counties, they are often overflowed.

The Cambridgeshire Fens contain many hills, some rising to 100ft above sea level, which literally became islands during the winter months. These hills are outcrops of green sandstone. In 731, the historian Bede reported that Ely was 'surrounded on all sides by sea and fens ... an island surrounded by water and marshes'.

HEREWARD THE WAKE

The Cambridgeshire Fens provided an ideal landscape for Saxon natives to resist the Norman invasion from 1066 onwards, and it was from some of these settlements that Hereward the Wake made his stand against the invaders.

Very little is known about the historical figure behind the legend of Hereward and the various medieval accounts are sometimes contradictory. It is not even known for certain what 'Wake' means; it is usually supposed to mean 'watchful', but it may also have been a name retrospectively applied to him by the Wake family, which inherited some of his lands. He first appeared on the national scene in 1070 when the Danish king Sweyn Estrithson sent an army to the Isle of Ely to assist the Fenlanders in their fight against the Norman occupiers. Hereward used these soldiers to storm Peterborough Abbey, which he then sacked, supposedly to safeguard its holy treasures. According to one medieval source, Hereward later returned them after he had had a vision of St Peter; according to another, the cathedral's treasures were shipped off to Denmark.

King William sent an army to crush the rebels and in 1071 Hereward's army made a last stand just outside Ely itself. The Normans began the attack by making a frontal assault along a mile-long timber causeway, but this sank under the weight of all the Norman armour and horses. The Normans then tried to intimidate the English into surrender with a witch, who cursed them from the top of a wooden tower, but Hereward started a fire that destroyed the tower with the witch still in it. Eventually, the Normans bribed the local monks to tell them about a safe route across the Fens, which resulted in Ely's capture. Legend says that Hereward escaped with some of his followers, to continue his armed resistance.

THE MEDIEVAL FENS

During the Middle Ages, the Isle of Ely was a Liberty of the Bishop, which meant that the Bishop and his officers exercised many powers that elsewhere in England were reserved to the King. The Bishop of Ely could, for example, arrange for criminals to be arrested and imprisoned, and he had authority to gather men together to become soldiers for the King's armies. Any court case which involved a resident of the Isle of Ely could, in theory, be transferred to the Bishop's Court, no matter which court in the land the case had originated in. During the early Middle Ages, the Isle was even exempt from central government taxation, and it did not contribute towards the Danegeld, but the taxation perk was removed during the taxation reforms of the thirteenth century.

The reason why the Isle's government was distinct was because its settlements were so cut off from the rest of the country by water. It was much more efficient for the inhabitants of the Isle to be ruled locally by the Bishop than for the King to try to rule them from London.

DRAINING THE FENS

The Romans were the first to have the vision and the capability to drain the Fens and they started to do so, building some canals and even constructing a huge bank between Wisbech and Walsoken. The climate also seems to have been warmer and drier during the Roman period, so the Fens may not have suffered as much from flooding as they were to do later. The Roman schemes were abandoned when they left and for many centuries afterwards nothing was done. During the Middle Ages most of the Isle of Ely's fenland was owned by just a handful of monasteries, which could easily have come together to arrange full drainage if they had wanted to do so, but it appears that they did not. The Dissolution of the Monasteries in the 1530s then broke up these large landholdings into hundreds of much smaller ones, which made the problem seem intractable.

Interest in land drainage was renewed during the later sixteenth and seventeenth centuries. In 1570, a particularly high tide broke through the Roman bank and flooded East Anglia as far as Bedfordshire, destroying many properties. Further bad floods occurred in 1598. These disasters not only prompted consideration about how best to prevent any similar floods in the future, but it also made some investors start to calculate how much profit could be made if a full drainage scheme was carried out and the land transformed into grazing pasture for sheep and cattle. In 1631, the fourth Earl of Bedford and thirteen other 'Adventurers' grouped their funds together to pay for initial drainage work and to appoint Dutchman Cornelius Vermuyden as their engineer. They were called Adventurers because they were adventuring their money, putting their own cash at risk on a scheme which may or may not have brought profit.

The Fens at this time only had a small population, so there was not enough local manpower to carry out the work. The Adventurers employed many prisoners of war from Holland and Scotland to cut a 21 mile-long drain from Earith to Denver, into which the water of the River Ouse was diverted. Work was completed in 1637, but the new drain did not have enough capacity and it burst its banks in its very first year. Work on improving the scheme had not progressed very far when the Civil War broke out and engineering work was halted.

In 1651 the Adventurers started work again and a second, much wider drain was cut parallel to the first one. The new channel was called the New Bedford River or, more simply, the Hundred Foot River because it was 100ft wide. The earlier 1630s channel was called the Old Bedford River or the Seventy Foot River. Barrier banks were built along the outsides of each river to trap any flood water in the space or 'washes' between the two channels. The Adventurers' ambition now was to drain the land so well that it could be used for arable farming as well as for livestock.

In 1653 the main fenland area was judged to be dry and land reclamation began. Surveyors divided thousands of acres of land into neat rectangular allotments, edged by drains, and these were distributed among the Adventurers. Nevertheless, there were still many pockets of fen and mere scattered around in areas where the water was so deep that it stayed flooded all through the year. Over the next two centuries, these too were drained and many other channels were cut, with names like the Forty Foot, the Twenty Foot and the Sixteen Foot Rivers. In other areas, existing rivers were realigned; the present course of the Nene from Peterborough to Guyhirn was cut in 1728 and the course of the Ouse between Ely and Littleport was straightened in 1827.

THE FEN MERES

At one time, there were many lakes or meres across the Fens such as Ramsey Mere, Ugg Mere, Trundle Mere, and Benwick, Stretham, Soham and Willingham Meres.

The largest was **Whittlesey Mere**. It was the largest natural lake in England outside the Lake District; 1,600 acres or 2.5 square miles in area, it may have expanded to 3,000 acres in winter and it may have been even larger before the drainage of the Fens began. It had an attractive shoreline, home to many types of wildlife – swallowtail butterflies, rare moths and exotic flowers. Many types of bird such as bittern and marsh harrier were common here before the mere was drained and subsequently disappeared. The poet John Clare used to walk from his home in Helpston just to admire the ferns on the shores of Whittlesey Mere. The mere was also used for fishing and for moving bulky goods such as building stone around.

The waters were used for regattas and 'water picnics'. On public holidays people would flock to the mere, where there were amusements laid on and even a bandstand. The mere was, however, subject to freakish storms that seemed to blow up regardless of the weather. Lord Orford, who embarked on a sailing trip around the Fens in the 1770s with nine small sailing ships, encountered one of these 'water quakes', as they were known locally, in July 1774 and reported in his diary that the ladies were quite seasick.

Soham Mere had been drained in 1664 and as the Fens around Whittlesey Mere were drained the mere itself became shallower, so when William Wells of Holmewood Hall proposed draining the whole Mere this was accepted. The development of steam pumps made this possible; the new pumps could lift 16,000 gallons a minute. The group of local landowners who funded the drainage made big profits when the land was first converted to farmland (3,500 acres of it) even though this was a monumental task, much of the digging being done by hand. By the 1880s though the collapse of corn prices made the whole area less profitable.

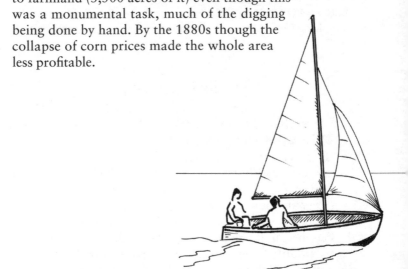

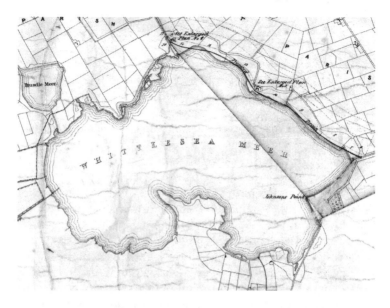

When the mere was drained, the wreck of several sunken boats were discovered, including a prehistoric canoe. A variety of interesting objects were recovered – such as an amount of silver from Ramsey Abbey, which included the Ramsey Censer (a small incense boat) now housed at the Victoria and Albert Museum. This was made around the time of Henry VIII, just before the Dissolution. Large building stones that were obviously being transported across the mere were also found at the bottom. People came from miles around to grab what they could once the drainage neared completion. Hundreds of tons of fish were caught and taken away. Thousands more were left to die and rot where they lay. Skulls of wild boar, a wolf and a whale were also found in the mud.

THE DRAINAGE ENGINES

When a peat bog dries out it shrinks, compacts and blows away in strong winds. As a consequence, the ground level gets lower and lower. When it was first drained, the ground level in the Cambridgeshire Fens fell dramatically (as much as 6ft in six years) and today the Fenland countryside is now much lower than the rivers which drain it to the sea. Excess water needs to be drained upwards, from ground level up into the rivers, so that the water can ultimately make its way to the sea.

Originally, horses and windmills were used to pump water upwards but as the ground level fell yet further it became obvious that only steam-powered pumps had enough power. One of these engines, the Stretham engine of 1831, is now preserved near Wicken Fen. By 1850 at least forty-eight steam engines were operating pumps across the Fens. During the twentieth century, diesel engines replaced the steam ones, especially during the Second World War when there was immense pressure to increase agricultural productivity as much as possible. Today, drainage is carried out by electric pumps, housed within small sheds that seem so insignificant that few people notice them as they drive past, yet without these pumps the Fens would flood within months.

HOLME POST

It is interesting that the original Adventurers did not realise that the peat would shrink after the land was drained. They were under the impression that drainage would be a one-off event. People were therefore rather bemused to see the drainage ditches get shallower and shallower and some thought that the bottoms of the ditches were somehow rising up. It was not until the 1660s that it was first suggested that the ground itself was sinking, but even then this was believed to be just a temporary event. The full extent of the shrinkage would not be understood for many years. Only in the early nineteenth century did the penny drop that the peat would continue to disappear in the winds, year by year, until the underlying clay was reached. It was this realisation that prompted the erection of the Holme Post.

In 1848, a timber post was embedded in the peat about half a mile from the edge of Whittlesey Mere in the parish of Holme. The base of the post was laid on the underlying clay layer, about 22ft down, and the top of the post was cut level with the peat surface. The mere was drained shortly afterwards and very soon observers could see the peat surface start to contract downwards as it dried out, revealing more and more of the post.

The original timber post was replaced in 1851 by a cast-iron one, which may have originally come from the Crystal Palace in London. It is this post that is still standing today. As the years have rolled by, more and more of the post has become visible above the remaining peat. By 2015, the ground level had shrunk over 13ft (about 4m) from the top of the post.

THE FEN BLOW

When winds blow from the east, there is nothing to stop them between Siberia and the Fens. In spring, if a strong wind blows across the flat land before the crops are established it can pick up dust and soil like a sandstorm. The sky can turn dark and young crops can be ruined. This is known as a Fen Blow. These conditions can make for poor visibility and difficult driving conditions. During the Fen Blow of April 2013, one motorist described it as 'like driving through Marmite'.

THE FUTURE OF FARMING IN THE FENS?

As the peat dries out it shrinks and blows away. This cannot continue indefinitely because one day in the future there will be no more peat fields left and the underlying clay will form the ground surface. It has been calculated that since 1850 about 84 per cent of the peat stock in the Fens has disappeared, so it is clear that the end of the peat is not far off.

A 2017 report, co-authored by Anglia Ruskin University, suggested that East Anglia could experience dustbowl conditions within the medium-term future, but a lot depends on what sort of climate the Fens will face over the next few decades. The worst case, which envisages an increasing number of hot, dry summers, suggests that the peat soil layer may completely disappear within thirty years. On the other hand, if summers do not worsen then the peat soil may still have eighty years or so left. Either way, it seems likely that some people alive today will see the end of peat agriculture in the Cambridgeshire Fens during their lifetimes.

EELS AND WILD-FOWLING

Catching eels and shooting wildfowl is a traditional part of Fen life, and indeed Ely gets its name from the number of eels caught there (Elge meaning eel district or eel island). Basket making from the many willow trees that grew in the Fens was a major

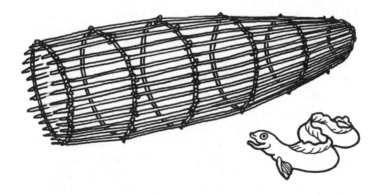

industry and eel traps known as griggs were commonly made from the stripped and woven willows branches or osiers.

Wild-fowlers paddled about lying flat in punts and developed long cannon-like guns that were mounted in the boat. These punt guns could be up to 2m long and one shot would kill dozens of birds.

FEN TIGERS

The Fenmen who made their living fishing, catching eels and wild-fowling, with their animals grazing on the common land, opposed the changes made during the drainage and conversion to arable land and they fought against it 'like tigers', sabotaging the ditches and so on. This is the origin of the name 'Fen Tiger' for the people of the Fens.

More recently, the name 'Fen Tiger' has been associated with a big cat, first spotted near Cottenham in 1982. Since then, there have been numerous sightings of a large black panther-like creature roaming around the Fens. This is believed to be a real big cat, not to be confused with the ghostly apparition of legend – Black Shuck. Shuck is the legendary descendant of the Hound of Odin, the great war dog of the Norse raiders. Legend says that if you see Black Shuck, or Old Shuck as he is known in the Fens, your number is up. (In Lincolnshire, however, he is seen not as a figure of fear, but as a protector of women and girls in lonely lanes.) A ghostly black dog with glowing red eyes, one of the earliest reported sightings was at Peterborough Abbey, recorded in the Peterborough Chronicle in the 1100s.

Littleport is home to two separate ghostly dog stories.

W.H. Barrett tells of a dog that haunted the area after being killed saving a local girl from the attentions of a lustful friar, whilst Enid Porter, curator of the Cambridge Folk Museum, tells of a dog being heard and sensed along the A10. Local legend says that the ghostly dog was awaiting its master, who had been drowned in the nearby river.

THE FEN SKATERS

Another popular pastime on Whittlesey Mere had been ice-skating. When the Dutch engineers came to Cambridgeshire in the seventeenth century they brought their ice skates with them and soon the sport of fen skating took off here. Skating was a popular pastime across the Fens. Winters were colder then and large expanses of flood water, as well as the rivers, could freeze solid during a cold spell. Areas such as Huntingdon Racecourse (in those days it was on Portholme Meadow) and Grantchester Meadows were flooded to form skating grounds and contests were held all across the Fens, with thousands coming to watch.

Many of these fen skaters became famous for their exploits. Some had nicknames like 'Turkey' Smart and 'Gutta-Percha' See. (Gutta-percha is a tough plastic substance made from the latex of a Malaysian tree, used in the manufacture of a variety of items, from golf balls to picture frames, but is now usually only used in dentistry.) Skaters would travel long distances to take part in races, thinking nothing of skating from St Ives to Wisbech, competing and then returning the same day. In 1895, Charles Tebbutt skated 83 miles in nine hours. In the races, competitors could reach speeds of 15 to 20mph.

The sport of Bandy, a type of ice hockey using a ball instead of a puck, also became popular in the Cambridgeshire Fens. The first recorded game was in the Great Freeze of 1813/14, although it had probably been played before. Charles Tebbutt of the Bury Fen Bandy Club, based at Bluntisham, drew up a set of rules for the game and introduced it to the Netherlands and Sweden. It is still extensively played in Scandinavian countries and Russia. Tebbutt's bandy stick may still be seen at the Norris Museum in St Ives.

A RESCUE FROM THE FENS

One Sunday afternoon in February 1851, a cottager's son was out bird-scaring near Holme. Around the drained bed of the mere there was an area of thick reeds about half a mile wide, the reeds growing to a height of 14ft or more. The boy walked too far into the reeds and suddenly found himself sinking into the bed of the mere, until he was up to his armpits in mud with his feet standing on the underlying peat. Trapped, he stayed there all through the night. He could clearly hear the bells of Conington church ringing each hour and even the trains of the Great Northern Railway, but no one heard his cries for help.

The next morning, he saw labourers in the distance but he was too cold to make any cry. At about ten o'clock he heard one labourer passing very close by on the other side of the reed bed, but the boy was powerless to call out and the sound died away. The boy thought his last hope had gone. Then suddenly the reeds opened and the man emerged. With great difficulty, he managed to extricate the boy, who had been trapped in the mud for nineteen hours. The man carried him home, 'much to the surprise of his parents, who had accepted his disappearance very philosophically, and had accounted for his absence by the gratuitous supposition that he had gone to the neighbouring village of Sawtry to see his grandmother who had kept him for the night'.

HOLME FEN SPITFIRE

In 2015, the remains of Spitfire X4593 were excavated from Holme Fen, almost seventy-five years after it had crashed there on 22 November 1940. The aircraft with pilot Harold Penketh at the controls nosedived at 300mph into the fen and sank into the peaty soil. The body of 20-year-old Pilot Officer Penketh, who had been stationed at nearby RAF Wittering, was recovered from the aircraft and returned to his home town of Brighton, but the wreck was left in the huge crater it had created. The remains of the aircraft were located after a geophysical survey of the area in August 2015.

The Bedfordshire, Cambridgeshire and Northamptonshire Wildlife Trust, in partnership with Oxford Archaeology East, excavated the Spitfire before the area was returned to its natural wetland state as part of the Great Fen Project. The propeller and parts of the engine and cockpit were discovered more than 6m down, as well as personal items such as a cigarette case, flying helmet and watch belonging to the pilot.

A memorial stone to Pilot Officer Penketh was unveiled at Holme Fen in September 2016.

WICKEN FEN AND THE GREAT FEN PROJECT

Since the 1630s, more than 99 per cent of the original fen wetlands has been lost to agriculture, yet a few scattered undrained areas still remain, most notably Wicken Fen, today a National Trust property. Wicken Fen is a nature reserve of such significance that it is protected internationally under the Ramsar wetlands protection scheme, but it is worth noting that the fen is not 'wild' in any meaningful sense. Although it looks and feels natural, its appearance is the result of many years of human management, and the National Trust continually ensures that the flora and fauna living there stays in balance. Because it was never drained, Wicken Fen is now higher than all the agricultural land surrounding it and water needs to be artificially pumped into the fen to prevent it drying out.

The National Trust has a very long-term vision to expand Wicken Fen. When Charles Rothschild first gave the fen to the Trust in 1899 it covered about 800 acres. The plan is to create, over the next century, a fenland area of over 20 square miles, to be achieved by purchasing much of the neighbouring farmland as it comes on to the market. Some land has already been bought and Wicken Fen is seeing increased numbers of birds including bitterns, marsh harriers, buzzards and short-eared owls.

Other patches of natural fenland include Woodwalton Fen and Holme Fen, near the location of the old Whittlesey Mere. In 1999, the Great Fen Project was launched with the aim of linking these two sites together and thereby protect the plants and animals there from nearby development. Woodwalton Fen is another Ramsar site of international significance while Holme Fen is the largest silver birch wood in southern England. In 2007, the Great Fen Project partners were awarded £7.2 million from the Heritage Lottery Fund, allowing the acquisition of 3,200 acres around Holme Fen.

The long-term aim of the Great Fen Project is to create a large haven for wildlife of about 14 square miles between Huntingdon and Peterborough. Not only will the new haven protect threatened wildlife but it will open new opportunities for recreation, education, tourism and business and its flora will help soak up carbon dioxide in the air, preventing the release of an estimated 325,000 tonnes of carbon dioxide every year.

THE FENLAND POMPEII: MUST FARM NEAR WHITTLESEY

In 1999 a local archaeologist noticed wooden posts sticking out of the mud at the edge of a quarry near Whittlesey. Evaluation of the site in 2006 revealed the remains of a Bronze Age settlement, built between 1000 and 800 BC. The houses had been built on piles, lifting them above a slow-moving river below. At some point, a catastrophic fire broke out, which destroyed the village but miraculously preserved many of the objects for us to find some 3,000 years later. The ferocious fire caused the settlement to collapse and sink into the silt at the bottom of river below. The degree of preservation gives a unique insight in to the life of this small Bronze Age community.

There were some truly amazing discoveries including pottery, in common with most archaeological sites, but a bowl discovered at Must Farm still contained the remains of the meal that was in it, as well as the spoon. Pieces of clothing made 3,000 years ago had survived due to the process of charring and water-logging. Analysis showed that these textiles were not made from animal skins, but from plant fibres.

One of the first discoveries made in 2011 was eight Bronze Age log boats found buried along the old course of the River Nene. One of the boats was 30ft (9m) long. They were taken to another important local archaeological site, Flag Fen, for conservation.

A full excavation, in 2015-16, by the University of Cambridge Archaeological Unit funded by Historic England and the owners of the site, Fonterra, discovered still more treasures which give a unique insight into life in the Bronze Age, including a large collection of domestic metalwork, beads, pottery, wattle panelling and textiles, as well as an almost complete wheel. Archaeologists also discovered the most complete Bronze Age dwellings ever found in Britain and a raised wooden walkway crossing the fen.

Cambridge University Archaeology Unit Manager David Gibson said, 'Usually at a Bronze Age site you find pits and post-holes. But this time so much more has been preserved – we can actually see everyday life during the Bronze Age.'

FEN PROVINCIALISMS

In the early volumes of *Fenland Notes and Queries* S. Egar gathered together many of the local words or expressions he had heard in the Fens. 'I have heard them chiefly from the lips of aged cottagers, fishermen, fowlers and workers in the fens, with whom my business has brought me very much in contact.' Some of Egar's words seem today to be not very provincial at all, such as 'batch' for a group of items, 'bunny' for rabbit, or 'new fangled' for newfangled, but some are highly evocative expressions from the local dialect. Here is a selection of some of the more striking.

arsy varsy:	vice versa
boke:	to vomit
butty:	a friend or companion ('a term much used among navvies')
cag mag:	bad or inferior meat
clung:	heavy, tough ('this land ploughs up very clung')
corned:	to be the worse for drink
cow lady:	a ladybird

fen nightingale:	frog
fullock:	used of shears that are prevented from cutting by earth ('I can't get on, on account of the sand: the shears fullock at it so')
go to Guyhirn:	an expression of derision
ho-go:	a vile smell
kicky:	showy
mog:	to move on
noodles:	people of weak intellect
ochre:	money
odling:	peerless, without equal
outner:	a stranger or foreigner
pink:	a chaffinch
quacken:	to choke or suffocate
rack-a-pelt:	an idle, troublesome vagabond
rafty:	rancid
ramper:	a raised road
scradge:	to raise and strengthen a fenland bank with any loose material within reach
scrat:	a hermaphrodite, used of cattle
shatteral:	a broken-down person or animal
slommacking:	awkward, blundering, clumsy
slunt:	abrupt, without manners

5

FESTIVALS AND FAIRS

Cambridgeshire has hosted many fairs and festivals over the centuries. Here are some of the most famous or significant, arranged in the order in which they were first set up.

ST IVES EASTER FAIR

In the year 1110, Henry I granted Ramsey Abbey the right to hold an annual fair every Easter in the village of Slepe. The Abbey had its own little church at Slepe, which was dedicated to St Ive, a bishop of Persia, and so the fair was known as St Ive's fair. It became so successful that the name of the fair soon became the name of the village.

The fair reached its peak during the thirteenth century when it hosted visiting traders from France and Belgium, dealing in cloth, wool, animal skins, furs and canvas. Henry III purchased so many robes there for his royal household that he requested the Prior of St Ives to provide a separate house for them within the grounds of the Priory. Goldsmiths are known to have attended the fair in 1278 and it was common for jewels to be traded there. At its zenith, St Ives' Easter Fair was one of the largest fairs in the whole of England.

The fair's strength, the presence of traders from the Continent, also proved its weakness. The outbreak of the Hundred Years' War in 1337 made it difficult for European merchants to attend, so they started to stay away. In 1341, the Easter Fair's merchants were robbed and held to ransom by a gang of criminals, which cannot have done anything for the fair's reputation. By 1363, the townsmen of Huntingdon were trying to claim, wrongly, that no fair had been held at St Ives for twenty years, but certainly the fair was a shadow of its former self. By 1511, it was a simple livestock and entertainment fair and its date had been moved from Easter to Whitsun.

The largest fair in St Ives today is the Michaelmas Fair, which takes place over three days beginning on the second Monday in October. This fair dates back rather tenuously to at least the early fourteenth century, when a new fair, smaller than the Easter one, was set up in St Ives on St Lawrence's Day in August. By the time of the Dissolution of the Monasteries its date appears to have shifted to Michaelmas.

REACH FAIR

This annual fair, originally held on Rogation Monday in May, is first mentioned in a charter of King John of 1201. Control of the fair was exercised by the borough of Cambridge, which, until the Dissolution of the Monasteries, took two-thirds of the income from the fair tolls, while the Prior of Ely took the other third. After the Dissolution, the borough took everything, but by then the fair was already in decline anyway. During the Middle Ages, Reach Fair had been a place where stocks of iron, steel and timber could be bought, but by 1432 it was reduced to just selling horses. During the nineteenth century, Reach Fair was famous more for its entertainment value than for its commercial activity, which was noted as being merely 'trifling'. It attracted many showmen and dancers and from the 1850s there was even a photographer.

The fair still takes place and is now held on Bank Holiday Monday. A custom is for the Mayor of Cambridge to scatter pennies into the crowd for children, this money coming from the income that the Corporation of Cambridge receives from the rent of Reach village green. In 2001, to mark the 800th anniversary of Reach Fair, a plaque commemorating the 1201 charter was unveiled on Hill Farm.

It is believed that Reach Fair has only been cancelled twice since 1201, both occasions being during the Civil War.

STOURBRIDGE FAIR

In 1211, Cambridge's Leper Hospital was granted by royal charter the right to hold an annual fair every 14 September. The Leper Hospital was in an excellent location for such a fair, as it was next to a broad field where one of the main roads out of Cambridge crossed the river Cam, over a bridge called Steresbrigg, from the number of cattle that used to be driven across it. The Leper Hospital closed in 1279 but by then the fair had become so popular that the Corporation of Cambridge stepped in and took it over.

During the Middle Ages, the fair was the largest in Europe. Traders and customers met to buy and sell the widest range of goods imaginable, including silks, china, glass, silver, cloth, wool, hops, cheese, livestock and horses. Honor Ridout, in her excellent history of the fair, *Cambridge and Stourbridge Fair* (2011), says that it was possible to equip and furnish an entire house completely with purchases made there.

In 1724, Daniel Defoe published an account of his visit to Stourbridge Fair in his travelogue *A Tour through England and Wales*:

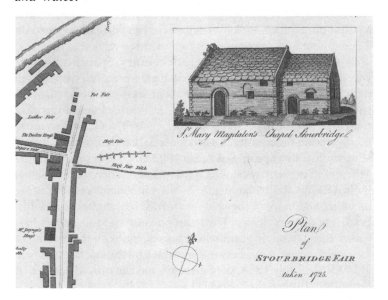

It is impossible to describe all the parts and circumstances of this fair exactly; the shops are placed in rows like streets, whereof one is call'd Cheapside; and here, as in several other streets, are all sorts of trades, who sell by retail, and who come principally from London with their goods; scarce any trades are omitted, goldsmiths, toyshops, brasiers, turners, milliners, haberdashers, hatters, mercers, drapers, pewterers, china-warehouses, and in a word all trades that can be named in London; with coffee-houses, taverns, brandy-shops, and eating-houses innumerable, and all in tents and booths.

As Defoe described, Stourbridge Fair was more like a temporary town than a fair. Every 24 August, by town proclamation, Stourbridge field was taken over by the fair's organisers, who pegged out where all the booths would go. These booths were arranged in streets (called 'Garlic Row', 'Cheese Row' and so on). They were sturdy structures, made of timber with steeply pitched roofs and often including a bedroom at the back. Gravel was spread out in front of the booths and open areas were marked out for livestock and for bulky wholesale products. Less well-off traders lived in tents or under their carts. A Maypole was erected, theatrical plays were put on for entertainment and a pulpit put up for Sunday sermons. The fair formally opened on 7 September and continued for two or three weeks.

By the middle of the eighteenth century, Stourbridge Fair was in decline. By then many tradesmen were preferring to sell their goods from their own permanent shops rather than from temporary stalls and the creation of the new canal and turnpike road network meant that it was much easier than before to move goods around the country. The commercial need for a large annual fair therefore disappeared. A fire in 1802 killed four people during a theatrical performance, which led to a permanent theatre being built within Cambridge itself. As the nineteenth century wore on, more and more of the field was turned over to housing, kilns, brick pits or the railway. The main purpose of Stourbridge Fair was reduced to buying and selling horses, but with the coming of the motor car, even this became unviable and the last fair was held in 1933. On 5 July 1934, the Borough issued an official notice that formally abolished Stourbridge Fair.

Since 2004 the fair has been commemorated on 11 September each year at the old Leper Chapel, which still stands in Cambridge.

MIDSUMMER FAIR

The year 1211 was a bumper year for Cambridge fairs because not only did King John grant Stourbridge Fair to the Leper Hospital but he also gave to the canons of Barnwell Priory the right to hold an annual fair on a piece of land called Green Croft, which would later be called Midsummer Common. In 1229, the fair was regulated to last four days, beginning on the Feast of St Etheldreda, specifically 22–25 June. By 1506, the Corporation of Cambridge had taken over the fair completely from the Priory and it became a major event in the civic calendar, with the Mayor, aldermen and college fellows dressing up in their formal robes to attend. During the eighteenth century, the fair stretched to a fortnight and so much china was bought and sold that it was called Pot Fair.

Midsummer Fair declined in commercial importance during the nineteenth century and in 1850 was reduced from a fortnight to its original four days, but its value as entertainment grew. In 1714, the fair is recorded as including a rope dancer, a giant, a dwarf, three-legged cats and dancing dogs. Steam engines first appeared in 1870 and soon these were powering merry-go-rounds and other fairground attractions. The fair still takes place each year on Midsummer Common.

SHAKESPEARE AT THE GEORGE, HUNTINGDON

The George Hotel in Huntingdon is first mentioned in the 1572 borough survey and has since been one of the town's most important inns. Charles I used it as his headquarters when the Royalist army occupied Huntingdon in 1645 and the Duke of Manchester later used it as a meeting point for his Light Horse Volunteer Brigade.

The George has a long history of staging plays, even before a proper theatre was built in the town in 1801. The tradition died out but it was revived in 1959 with a production of Shakespeare's *The Taming of the Shrew*, staged in the George's seventeenth-century courtyard. Productions of Shakespeare's plays have been held in the courtyard ever since and annually since 1978. The productions are run by a group of trustees and the entire cast and crew are volunteers.

WHITTLESEA STRAW BEAR FESTIVAL

The earliest reference to this custom dates from the late nineteenth century. On the Tuesday following Plough Monday, one of the community would dress completely in straw and then be led around Whittlesea on a chain lead, acting like a bear and dancing for money, beer or food. Although it was made from the finest straw available in the parish, the costume must have been very uncomfortable and the poor victim could hardly see out of his straw helmet. The local police banned the custom in 1909 as it must have been quite intimidating for locals, who were expected to donate the gifts.

In 1980, the straw bear custom was revived by the Whittlesea Society and the festival has continued annually ever since. The bear suit is now constructed far more comfortably, with the straw fixed onto a removable metal frame. The bear forms the centrepiece of a procession of performers, musicians and Molly dancers who journey through the town, accompanied by a decorated plough. Local pubs put on live traditional music during the day and a barn dance rounds off the evening. The procession takes place on the second Saturday in January. On the Sunday, the bear suit is publicly burnt, a suitably *Wicker Man*-style ending to the festival.

CHEESE ROLLING AT STILTON

In 1959, the village of Stilton was bypassed by the A1 and its pubs and inns lost much passing trade. One pub landlord started rolling a Stilton cheese back and forth outside his pub in an attempt to attract custom. What started perhaps in desperation has, over the years, developed into Stilton's main annual festival, sporting live music, Molly dancing, fairground rides and a Maypole. The centrepiece, of course, is the cheese rolling itself, which attracts up to 2,000 visitors from across the country every May bank holiday. The starting line is outside the Bell Inn and the Angel pub, where a circular wooden 'cheese' is placed. Real cheese cannot be used because it simply would not survive the ordeal of being rolled along the ground. Teams of four, often in fancy dress relevant to the theme of that year's festival, then roll the 'cheese' about 200 yards along the street to the village crossroads in a knock-out competition.

Stilton cheese itself is not made locally, but can only be made in Derbyshire, Nottinghamshire and Leicestershire.

WISBECH ROSE FAIR

Wisbech's Rose Fair began in 1963, when local rose growers sold rosebuds to the public in aid of the restoration fund for St Peter and Paul's church. In the half century since then, the fair has grown into an annual town event and has become one of the country's finest flower festivals. Many local churches and organisations stage events and provide stalls selling local produce, plants and crafts, all to raise money for a variety of causes. The fair is held in late June or early July.

CAMBRIDGE FOLK FESTIVAL

In 1964, Cambridge City Council decided to hold a music festival. Inspired by the jazz festivals of America, Ken Woollard, organiser of the very first folk festival in 1965, had the good fortune to include a young Paul Simon on the bill. Since then, the festival has grown in size and importance and has become one of the most famous folk music festivals in the world, helped by its rather broad definition of 'folk', which includes gospel, blues, jazz and even some pop. The festival provides an opportunity for visitors to hear excellent musicians in intimate surroundings and often to jam with them in informal sessions. Headline acts have included some of the most famous names in folk, including Joan Baez, Fairport Convention, The Proclaimers, Van Morrison, Sinead O'Connor, Beth Orton, Wilko Johnson, Joan Armatrading and Jake Bugg. The festival is held over a long weekend each summer on the site of Cherry Hinton Hall on the south side of Cambridge.

STRAWBERRY FAIR, CAMBRIDGE

Strawberry Fair is a one-day music and arts event that takes place annually on Midsummer Common in Cambridge on the first Saturday in June. The very first Strawberry Fair was organised in 1974 by Cambridge University students as an alternative to the more official college May balls. It included clowns, wholefood stalls and a stage for musical and comedy performers. It proved a success and the event was repeated in 1975, with a Chinese dragon in attendance and 2,000 people attending. The festival continued to grow in scale and at its peak in the 1990s it was attracting over 50,000 people. Its association with political protest and New Age hippy-style beliefs and aesthetics took hold in the 1980s as a reaction against the Thatcher government.

In 2010, the police appealed against the fair's licence from the City Council and for the only time in its history the fair did not go ahead. This 'year off' gave the organisers an opportunity to rethink the layout, size and focus of Strawberry Fair, so that when it returned in 2011, it had a greater emphasis on enjoyable activities for children and young adults. The fair continues to provide a venue for local bands and, since 2004, has promoted local film-makers too, so successfully in fact that since 2010 it has run a spin-off film festival called Strawberry Shorts.

The organisers of Strawberry Fair greatly value their independence and creativity. The fair therefore has no major sponsors or grant funding, but survives entirely on volunteer energy, contributions from local traders and income from events staged throughout the year, such as Cambridge Band Competitions, open mic nights and merchandise. It is thanks to the input of about 1,000 volunteers each year that Strawberry Fair has been able to remain free for all its visitors.

SOHAM PUMPKIN FAIR

The Pumpkin Fair has been running since 1975 and is held annually on the town's recreation ground on the last Saturday in September. The event is supported by the town council, local businesses, organisations and a team of dedicated volunteers, and it raises money for local charities. Attractions over the years have included a funfair, vintage vehicles, bygones and arena displays by local groups, but at its heart the fair is an opportunity for locals and visitors to show off the size of their home-grown vegetables or the height of their sunflowers. The main events, of course, are the pumpkin competitions, with categories ranging from 'Heaviest pumpkin grown by a Soham child' right up to 'Heaviest pumpkin grown in East Anglia'. In 2005, the Pumpkin Fair Committee went to Soham's proposed twin town of Andrézieux-Bouthéon in France to see its own pumpkin fair (or *Fête de la Courge*).

ARBURY CARNIVAL, CAMBRIDGE

The Arbury Carnival takes place in Arbury Town Park annually on the second Saturday in June and attracts up to 5,000 people. It was first held in 1977 to celebrate the Queen's Silver Jubilee. In October 2016, the carnival won a grant from the Big Lottery Fund to help make its 40th anniversary event in 2017 the largest ever.

ETHELDREDA CRAFT AND FOOD FAIR, ELY

The annual Etheldreda Craft and Food Fair takes place in June on Palace Green in front of Ely Cathedral. Its aim is to be a traditional English fair, with coconut shys, tombolas and strawberries and cream, with any profits going to the Ely Cathedral Choir Tour Fund. The fair's origins lie in the early 1990s as a little garden party held on the Open University's Degree Ceremony Day, but it grew over the course of the 1990s to become a proper fair, adopting the name of the founding abbess of Ely Cathedral.

EEL FESTIVAL, ELY

Ely's annual Eel Festival takes place over the first bank holiday weekend in May and celebrates the humble eel. Ely's Ellie the Eel heads the procession on Saturday from the cathedral down to the Waterside, where traditional events include throwing the (stuffed) eel and a chance to eat smoked and jellied eels. The procession follows the circular Eel Trail around the city's historic buildings, marked in the pavement by over seventy bronze eel plaques. The festival was first held in 2004 to mark the important role once played by the eel in Ely's history as a source of income and pride.

6

UP AND AWAY: FLYING IN CAMBRIDGESHIRE

THE EARLY DAYS OF FLYING

The first flight over Cambridge took place in 1783, when a balloon piloted by Mr Astley took off. Several more balloon ascents followed soon after, including one from Palace Green, Ely, in January 1785. Parker's Piece in Cambridge was used as an 'aerodrome' several times. It was here that Mr Green made an ascent in his Coronation Balloon at the Grand Fête in 1830. The most famous balloon flight was an ascent to mark the coronation of Queen Victoria at the huge feast given in 1838.

Ballooning 'took off' across the county with flights at Barnwell, Cheveley, Elsworth and Gamlingay. The first parachute jump in the county probably took place on 20 September 1889.

Cambridgeshire has been home to aeroplanes and airfields since flying began. The first aircraft construction took place at West Wratting Hall in 1867. The craft took ten years to complete and cost £1,000. It was called the Frost Ornithopter, but the engine was underpowered and the machine was abandoned. Another ornithopter, which had flapping wings that lifted it about 2ft off the ground, was built in 1905.

A 'Chesterton Biplane', which had been built in a barn near the Pike and Eel pub at Needingworth, was shown at May Week 1910.

There was also an early attempt at flying in Oakington, in 1910, when Grose and Fairley built a monoplane in a barn at Manor Farm in an attempt to win the *Daily Mail* £1,000 prize for flying 1 mile in a British plane – the flight trials were unsuccessful and the aircraft was disposed of.

FLYING AT PORTHOLME

Some of the earliest successful flights took place from Portholme, near Huntingdon. In a booklet entitled *Huntingdon the Aviation Centre*, published in May 1910, H. Massac Buist, author and noted motoring correspondent from the *Morning Post*, extolled the virtues of Portholme as a suitable venue for an 'aeroplaning ground'.

Portholme Meadow, said to be the largest in England, was held to be ideal for the purpose. Firstly, there was its size, 257 acres, large enough to give a circuit of almost 2 miles. It was also very flat, had no streams running across it nor any large trees or shrubs that would need clearing. There were no surrounding hills to cause erratic wind currents. Aeroplanes at the time were still frail craft, made from wood, canvas and wire, so a wind of 10 knots or so could make handling them almost impossible.

Portholme had been Huntingdon's racecourse and viewing stands for the flying races could be erected on the site of the old racecourse stands.

The clinching factor in Huntingdon's suitability as a potential aviation centre, however, was the proximity of the meadow to the railway. Trains could converge on Huntingdon from north, south, east or west, giving a potential catchment of 8 million people for important meetings (according to Buist). Both Huntingdon and Godmanchester railway stations were within five minutes' walk of Portholme. At this period not even all 'aeroplanists' were motorists and the general public certainly wouldn't have been. Very few people would have owned a motor car, so access to good railway connections was crucial. Despite all this, the attempt to set up an aviation course at Portholme failed.

Nevertheless, the meadow was still an ideal place for the early airmen to practise their flying. On 9 April 1910 James Radley made the first flight from Portholme, a straight hop of 100 yards. His aircraft had been brought in by rail in late March and wheeled through the streets before the wings were fitted.

On 20 April he recorded a flight of 16½ miles or ten circuits in 23 minutes 55 seconds (about 42mph). He flew at a height of around 40ft. His aircraft was a Bleriot monoplane.

Radley joined forces with William Rhodes-Moorhouse and together they set up a business designing and building aeroplanes in Huntingdon. Rhodes-Moorhouse was educated at Cambridge University, but he devoted himself to the world of engines, racing both cars and motorcycles. Will had a reputation as a fine, although not particularly successful, motor car driver and first appeared in Huntingdon as mechanic to James Radley.

In October 1911 Rhodes-Moorhouse flew the first aircraft to be seen in Peterborough, where he circled the Cathedral, and was back in Huntingdon in 37 minutes. Officials from Peterborough telephoned the aerodrome once the plane was on its return journey. There were free drinks in the George Hotel that evening.

In the same month, he flew over Cambridge, causing great excitement. Appearing from the Trumpington direction, he swooped down past the tower of the Catholic church, just cleared the houses in Regent Street and landed on Parker's Piece.

Rhodes-Moorhouse soon became celebrated as an aviator of great daring. He was the first person to turn off his engine in mid-air to see what would happen – fortunately he landed safely. He visited America, where he competed in race meetings and became the first man to fly through the archways of the Golden Gate Bridge in San Francisco.

AIRSHIPS

During the 1912 General Army Manoeuvres, a landing ground was established at the village of Hardwick. It was used by many well-known airmen, including Mr Geoffrey de Havilland. Also during the 1912 Manoeuvres, held near Cambridge, Army airships were seen flying around the southern part of the county. Airship *Beta II* landed at Jesus Grove and *Gamma II* landed at Kneesworth in 1913, while yet another airship was seen at Sutton near Ely, causing great excitement.

One of the last airships seen over the county was the famous *R101*, which passed over Cambridgeshire on its way from the base at Cardington in Bedfordshire to Sandringham. The *R101* was designed for passenger travel, but crashed in France a year later, killing most of those on board.

FIRST WORLD WAR AIRFIELDS IN CAMBRIDGESHIRE

It was during the First World War that flying became more commonplace over the county. It was originally a gentleman's occupation. Lieutenant Gathercole, a pilot of the Royal Flying Corps, landed in Cherry Hinton to visit relations at the Hall. The first aerial force to be deployed to France consisted of just 105 officers, sixty-three aircraft and ninety-five MT vehicles.

The Portholme Aerodrome Company began to build armoured cars, seaplanes and Sopwith Camels and Snipes. Many former Portholme fliers joined the Royal Flying Corps (RFC). William Barnes Rhodes-Moorhouse joined at the outbreak of war, officially enlisting on 24 August 1914 as a second lieutenant.

During the First Battle of Ypres, the RFC was called on to undertake a series of bombing raids to disrupt German troop movements to the front. Rhodes-Moorhouse was given the objective of the rail centre at Courtrai, 35 miles away in France. At 3.05 p.m. on 26 April 1915 he left on a single-handed bombing raid on Courtrai railway junction. After dropping the bombs, he was hit by a rifle bullet fired from the belfry of Courtrai church, which hit him in the thigh. Instead of landing to receive treatment for his wound, he decided to return to base. He ran into more gunfire and was hit again in the abdomen and hand. After flying back to base, he made his report but died the next day, 27 April 1915. He was 27 years old. His aircraft had ninety-five bullet and shrapnel holes in it. His body was returned to England and buried with full military honours. On 22 May 1915, the *London Gazette* reported the award of a posthumous Victoria Cross 'for conspicuous bravery', the first airman to win that distinction.

Moorhouse's son, also named William, became a pilot in the Second World War and was killed in the Battle of Britain in September 1940.

WYTON AIRFIELD

The small air force was expanded, but losses were considerable. New airfields were set up to train a new batch of pilots. Wyton was one of these airfields and a landing ground was established there in April 1916. After a few hours of advanced training, pilots often went straight to operational squadrons.

The basic requirements of training were:

- Flying 15 hours solo
- Flying a service aeroplane
- Flying cross-country for 60 miles, landing at two other locations under the supervision of an RFC officer

- Climbing to 6,000ft and staying there for at least 15 minutes, then landing within a circular mark, 50 yards in diameter
- Making two night landings, assisted by flares.

Wyton's role became that of a mobilisation station. No one wore the RFC uniform, but instead that of the regiment from which they had come; thus some wore cavalry breeches, some puttees, some stockings and gaiters and several wore kilts.

Over the next two to three years it grew to be a sizeable camp, the whole station covering 151 acres, 30 of which were occupied by buildings. Five hangars were built and huts for accommodation were set up on the opposite side of the Chatteris road. It could cater for three squadrons, but had a permanent staff of only three officers, six NCOs and twenty-one airmen. Strangely enough, the uneven clay soil at Wyton was not particularly good for flying as it tended to be dotted with small lakes after heavy rain. In the winter of 1917/18 only 52.9 per cent of the possible flying hours were actually suitable for flying.

After the war, the buildings at Wyton were reused as schools and businesses in Huntingdon. Some of them became a sanatorium for the treatment of TB, but were only deemed suitable for women and children!

Many airmen were lost over France, but accidents were common at home too, particularly as airmen liked to show off their planes to family and friends. On 23 September 1917 Norris Knight flew his Farman Shorthorn low over the houses in Filbert's Walk, St Ives. His relatives, the Harrisons, lived there. On the return to his base at Wyton, he clipped the trees in Barnes Walk, just behind the church, and nosedived into the garden of Barnes House. Due to the design of the Shorthorn, with its network of struts and wires and a top speed of 66mph, he emerged unscathed.

On 27 March 1918, 2nd Lieutenant Wastell from Wyton was killed when his aircraft, a De Havilland DH.6, flew into the spire of St Ives church. Considerable damage was done to the church, but no one else was injured. The spire of the church collapsed into the north aisle and the aircraft landed in the south aisle. It wasn't until 1923 that enough money was raised to start rebuilding the spire.

OTHER AIRFIELDS

Upwood, near Ramsey, was in use as a military landing ground in 1917 after land at Simmonds Farm was requisitioned. The first operational squadron arrived at Upwood in 1918, by which time five large hangars had been erected. It fell into disuse after the end of the war and the site reverted to farmland, but most of the buildings remained and were used as farm cottages. The five hangars were dismantled. When the RAF took the land back in 1935, a lot of the original First World War buildings still remained and were still in use in 1954 by the Royal Air Force.

The Royal Flying Corps also established an airfield near Old Weston in Huntingdonshire, in 1917. It was abandoned after the war and the buildings used by local farms. During the Second World War, RAF Molesworth was built in the same area.

Duxford opened in the early days of the RAF in 1919. Originally a training school, Duxford became a fighter squadron base in 1923.The fighters in those days were biplanes.

There was another First World War base at Fowlmere.

Cambridge airfield was also established early on as a flying school. It was originally set up at Whitehall by Arthur Marshall in 1929. That site has long since disappeared under a housing estate. The airfield transferred to its current site in 1937. For many years it had been home to the Cambridge University Air Squadron, which provided many of the RAF's pilots.

From December 1916, Stamford, the most northerly of Cambridgeshire's airfields, had housed a flight of the Home Defence Force anti-Zeppelin fighters. The Central Flying School moved there in 1924 and it has been in continuous service as RAF Wittering ever since.

THE THIRTIES

Several airfields were built in Cambridgeshire in response to the threat from the German Luftwaffe in the 1930s. Wyton has been a major station since 1936 and is one of the few still in operation today.

Upwood was reopened in 1937, despite the fact that the clay soil there meant the ground was almost always waterlogged or cracked. One of 52 Squadron's first missions from Upwood was to help in the search for the 72-year-old Duchess of Bedford, who had left Woburn flying her Gypsy Moth biplane. She took off in a snowstorm on a flight to view the Fens, but despite several days of searching she was never seen again.

Alconbury opened as a satellite ground for Upwood in May 1938. During the war, there was so much activity at Upwood that Alconbury became a station in its own right. Forty years later the roles were reversed and Upwood became a satellite for the USAF at RAF Alconbury.

The first contingent of RAF personnel arrived at Bassingbourn on 25 March 1938.

Waterbeach was one of the last permanent stations to be planned before the war and the last to open, in January 1941. The site is only 17ft above sea level, which wouldn't appear to be ideal for an airfield, but the site is well drained and didn't suffer from mud and standing water like many of the others.

Duxford has the honour of being the RAF's first Spitfire base. On 4 August 1938, the RAF's very first Spitfire began operations with No. 19 Squadron. By the outbreak of war in 1939, three Spitfire squadrons were based at Duxford alongside aeroplanes belonging to the Meteorological Flight and the Cambridge University Air Squadron. The Spitfire was described by *Flight* magazine as a 'poem of speed and precision' – at the time it was the fastest fighter in the world. R.J. Mitchell, the designer, was not impressed with the name of his revolutionary new plane. He called it the 'sort of bloody stupid name they would choose'.

WAR BEGINS

Just after noon on 3 September 1939, a Blenheim bomber of 139 Squadron flew the first operational sortie of the Second World War, 45 minutes after the Prime Minister's broadcast informing the nation that the country was at war. The plane photographed the German Navy at Wilhelmshaven. They failed to radio back the information as the radio set had frozen in the intense cold at 24,000ft. The aircraft landed safely just before 5 p.m.

Most of the thirty wartime airfields in Cambridgeshire were opened after war was declared, many as satellite grounds to the permanent stations. Alconbury and Warboys were attached to Upwood, Fowlmere and Snailwell to Duxford, Bourn to Oakington and Kimbolton to Molesworth.

By 1944, there were twenty-four operational airfields in Cambridgeshire: Alconbury, Bassingbourn, Bottisham, Bourn, Castle Camps, Duxford, Fowlmere, Glatton, Gransden Lodge, Graveley, Kimbolton, Little Staughton, Mepal, Molesworth, Oakington, Snailwell, Steeple Morden, Upwood, Warboys, Waterbeach, Witchford, Wittering, Wratting Common and Wyton. The skies would have throbbed with the sound of engines.

Peterborough (or Westwood), Sibson, Caxton Gibbet and Lord's Bridge were minor airfields or landing grounds. Lord's Bridge, near Barton, was mainly used as a bomb store. It would have made a prime target but, fortunately, was never attacked. Caxton Gibbet, on the other hand, was attacked by the Luftwaffe on six occasions. Two civilian workers from Marshall's were killed in one of the raids, but otherwise there was little damage. Peterborough, and later Sibson, were used mainly for training.

Strangely, Sibson is one of the county's few airfields still in use, as Peterborough Business Airport.

Somersham airfield was set up as a decoy for the major centre at Wyton, with dummy hangars and mock aircraft. Its simple grass runway was also used by the squadrons of the Special Operations Executive (SOE) to practise landing and taking off with agents.

Cambridge saw little operational action but was an important repair centre and training school. Young men arriving at flying school would be issued with their flying kit, which included leather helmet, earphones, inner garment of padded silk and wool, gauntlets, silk under-gloves and flying boots lined with lambswool – it was cold at altitude. The initial training course lasted eight weeks. The first training flight was in a Tiger Moth, a biplane with a top speed of 109mph. The skies around Cambridge literally buzzed with them.

Construction work went on everywhere. In the 1940s, most runways were still grass. The runway at Wittering needed to be extended, so the station commander negotiated a deal with the local landowner, the Marquis of Exeter, to give up the land. In return, the RAF purchased the potato crop that had already been planted there. The new extra-long runway was used for landing damaged aircraft. At Warboys the new runway was so long that the road to Huntingdon had to be closed and the traffic diverted. The A142 Ely to Chatteris road was also closed for much of the war as it ran straight through the airfield at Mepal.

Many aircrews had to live in makeshift buildings and tents. Wratting Common was 400ft above sea level, unusually high for Cambridgeshire and not particularly hospitable in winter. Bourn was described as 'a wasteland of mud and Nissen huts'.

THE PATHFINDERS

It is well known that Cambridgeshire was the headquarters of the RAF Pathfinder Force, a force made up of expert navigators who flew ahead of the main bombing force to identify and mark out the targets. The gallantry of the Pathfinders is legendary and their contribution to the war was immense.

The man chosen to lead the Pathfinders, an Australian, Don Bennett, was looking for a base with good communications and transport links and consistently above average weather conditions. He chose RAF Wyton. His second station was Oakington, both ready-made pre-war stations. Graveley and Warboys were the first two satellite stations. Later, Upwood, Bourn, Little Staughton and Gransden Lodge became Pathfinder stations, too.

Pathfinder headquarters were moved to Castle Hill House in Huntingdon – the Huntingdonshire District Council offices built in the grounds in the 1970s were named Pathfinder House in honour of the force.

One of the most dangerous missions was flying fast, stripped-back and unarmed Mosquitos over Europe to check the weather conditions. Many of these meteorological missions were flown from Wyton. During the course of the war, Wyton lost 218 aircraft. In the winter of 1943/44, it was estimated that a Pathfinder Force crew stood a 15 per cent chance of survival.

One of the most well-known Pathfinder commanders, Group Captain John Searby DSO, DFC was a local man, born in Whittlesey. It was he who directed the famous Peenemünde Raid on the German V2 rocket development site, for which he was awarded the DSO. He later became an air commodore.

Besides its Pathfinder duties, Graveley was used as a satellite to Tempsford, the base of the SOE. It spent most of the war dropping agents into occupied Europe and picking them up again, along with delivering supplies for the SOE and Resistance.

Graveley was also the test site for FIDO – the Fog Investigation Dispersal Operation. Many aircraft had crashed in the fog over East Anglia. Pipes with burners (6,900 of them) were placed along the runways, giving off bursts of intense heat that cleared the fog and enabled aircraft to land in poor visibility, which saved many lives. The first test produced so much flame that fire crews rushed to the scene. The scheme was ultimately used at fifteen airfields.

Little Staughton airfield could boast two VCs amongst the airmen who served there. Squadron Leader Robert A.M. Palmer VC DFC and Bar of 109 Squadron, who won his award for 'his record of prolonged and heroic endeavour', was killed in action on 23 December 1944, while Captain Edwin Swales VC DFC of the South African Air Force's 582 Squadron, the only South African to serve in the Pathfinder Force, also won his award posthumously: 'Intrepid in the attack, courageous in the face of danger, he did his duty to the last, and giving his life that his comrades might live,' Swales died in February 1945. Returning from having successfully directed a raid over Pforzheim near Stuttgart, he controlled the stricken aircraft for long enough for his crew to bail out, but he did not have time to follow them. In all, 200 airmen lost their lives whilst serving at Little Staughton.

THE FRIENDLY INVASION

Several overseas squadrons were based in the county: Canadians at Gransden Lodge, New Zealanders at Mepal and Wittering, and Belgians at Bottisham (they had a training school at Snailwell). Czechoslovakian pilots flew from Duxford during the Battle of Britain. There were fourteen Polish squadrons in all, with 17,000 officers and men. Nearly 2,000 of them were killed. One of the squadrons was at Snailwell.

The largest 'invasion force', however, came from America. In 1942, the USAAF 8th Air Force arrived in Cambridgeshire and took over Alconbury, Bassingbourn, Kimbolton, Molesworth and Glatton. Later, four fighter squadrons were established at Bottisham, Duxford, Fowlmere and Steeple Morden. Glatton was the only airfield in the country to be actually constructed by the Americans. Little Staughton was also briefly occupied by American forces.

Alconbury became the first base for the B-24 Liberator bombers. USAAF forces tended to give their planes special names such as *Evening Folks How Y'All*, *Hell's Hole*, *Eagle's Wrath* and *Shoo Shoo Baby* at Bassingbourn, and *Bugs Bunny* and *Flying Bison* at Molesworth.

The most famous aircraft of all was the *Memphis Belle*, another Bassingbourn B-17 Flying Fortress, which was the subject of a film documentary on the 8th Air Force. It was one of the first USAAF aircraft to complete twenty-five combat missions unscathed. The aircraft and crew returned to the USA

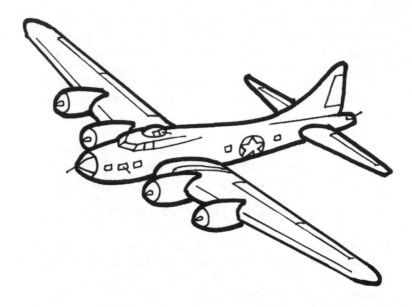

and made a fundraising tour. After the war, the aircraft was saved from the scrapyard and purchased by the city of Memphis and put on display there. The *Memphis Belle* was the subject of another film, the eponymous Hollywood movie made in 1990. It is now at the National Museum of the US Air Force in Ohio.

Molesworth was home to the 303rd Bombardment Group, the first 'Hell's Angels'. The entire unit was named for the first of its aircraft to get through twenty-five missions in one piece. When the group returned to California after the war, they liked the name so much they used it for the new groups of motorbike riders they were forming.

Screen idol (Captain) Clark Gable (then aged 41) flew his first mission with 303rd Group from Molesworth in 1943, making a propaganda film about air gunners called *Combat America*. Young war reporter Walter Cronkite was also based at Molesworth. He later became the anchorman for CBS news. Perhaps the most surprising name to be associated with 303rd Group is Goering, not the Nazi commander of the Luftwaffe, but his nephew, First Lieutenant Werner G. Goering, who flew B-17 bombers out of Molesworth.

Molesworth also had the distinction of generating more marriages between Americans and local girls (known as GI brides) than any other airbase in the whole of England, 400 in all.

Steeple Morden was a satellite for Bassingbourn, mainly used for practice landings, but it has several claims to fame. On 16 February 1941, a German Junkers Ju 88A aircraft landed there – the crew thought they were in France.

The USAAF Photographic Group arrived there on 2 November 1942. They were commanded by Elliott Roosevelt, son of the US President.

Pilots from Steeple Morden were involved in Operation *Frantic VII* to drop supplies to Polish Resistance fighters involved in the Warsaw Uprising.

US airbases attracted high-profile visitors. Glenn Miller and his band came to Steeple Morden in August 1944, while Bing Crosbie and Bob Hope entertained the troops at Bassingbourn.

OTHER MISSIONS

Not all the missions launched from Cambridgeshire involved death and destruction. At the end of April and early May 1945, crews from Witchford and Wratting Common were involved in Operation *Manna*, the airborne supply of food to starving people in west Holland. About 6,600 tons of food, sweets and tobacco were dropped in small bomb canisters without the use of parachutes. Over 2,800 Lancaster crews in total were involved in the operation.

A few days later, 115 Squadron crews from Witchford were involved in Operation *Exodus*, picking up Allied prisoners of war from Juvincourt airfield.

AFTER THE WAR

When the Second World War ended, most of Cambridgeshire's airfields began to revert to farmland or were left to slowly decay. Some of the old wartime buildings can still be seen today. Little Staughton is probably the best example, where the old control tower and runways still remain. Many are now only marked by a memorial stone, put up years later, like the ones at Witchford and Wratting Common.

The people of Great Gransden installed a beautiful memorial window in their church to commemorate those Canadian airmen who served at Gransden Lodge and gave their lives. It reads: 'The people of these villages cared for the Airmen who flew from RAF Gransden Lodge. They watched for them and prayed for them.' There is a Pathfinder Memorial window in Warboys church and a memorial window dedicated to 7 Squadron in Longstanton church.

Cambridge airfield made history when the ban on civilian flying was lifted in January 1946. The Mayor of Cambridge, Lady Bragg, became the first post-war civilian passenger, in the back seat of a Tiger Moth.

Marshall Aerospace has continued to operate the airfield in Cambridge with private charters and a limited number of scheduled passenger flights. The main business at Cambridge is the conversion, modification and maintenance of aircraft, mainly for the RAF, and a number of airlines, including Virgin and British Airways, as well as design and development. The training school is also still in operation.

Several airfields were kept on until the 1960s. Bourn was sold in 1961 and is now best known as the venue for a Bank Holiday market. In 1994, it had a brief moment in the spotlight when it featured in the Pink Floyd music video of *High Hopes*. Kimbolton and Warboys became training stations for the RAF. Warboys later became the home of the Bloodhound Air Defence System but closed in 1963.

After the war, Oakington became a flying training station and hundreds of pilots gained their wings there. In 1972 RAF Oakington was awarded the Honorary Freedom of the City of

Cambridge in recognition of the invaluable and distinguished services rendered by the Royal Air Force, the highest honour that can be bestowed by a city or borough.

Oakington was handed over to the Army soon after. The 1st Battalion of the Royal Anglian Regiment were based there from 1975. The airfield was subsequently taken over by the Home Office and between 2000 and 2010 some of the buildings were used as an immigration reception centre to process people who had entered the country illegally. Some 40,000 people passed through the centre in the first five years. The whole area is now being developed as the new town of Northstowe.

Waterbeach was also occupied by the Army after the war; the 39th battalion of the Royal Engineers arrived in 1966. The whole site closed in 2013 after seventy years of continuous military occupation and, like Oakington, is earmarked for a large housing development; a planning application was submitted in 2017.

Similarly, Bassingbourn was taken over by the Army as a training base in 1970. Directly after the war, the airfield had been used as a base for flying VIPs and government officials all over the world (they were usually picked up at Northolt as this was more convenient for London). Aircraft from Bassingbourn also took part in the Berlin Airlift. The Korean conflict and the general state of uncertainty had brought the Americans back to Bassingbourn in 1950 and 1951 and flying continued with Canberra bombers through the 1950s and '60s. Soon though, Bassingbourn's flying days were over and material from the subsidiary runways was used as hard core during the construction of the M11 motorway in the 1970s.

An unusual feature at the entrance to the barracks at Bassingbourn is the Changi Lychgate. It was originally built at Changi by British prisoners imprisoned by the Japanese and stood at the entrance to the cemetery where 400 POWs were buried. When the British garrison left Singapore, the gate was shipped back to England. As most of the Changi prisoners had been from East Anglia, it was re-erected at Bassingbourn in 1972 as a memorial to the men of 18th Division.

The airfield at Wittering became the country's premier fighter station. In 1969 it became the 'Home of the Harrier', the world's first VTOL (vertical take-off and landing) aircraft. The Harriers left in 2000, but the station still houses several different units and has been in almost continuous operation for over 100 years.

Alconbury ceased operations in 1945, but the Cold War brought it back to prominence and the USAF based many aircraft there, including Phantom reconnaissance jets and the Lockheed TR-1, a version of the U-2 spy plane.

In 1991, aircraft from Alconbury flew over 1,000 combat missions against Iraqi targets as part of Operation *Desert Storm*, destroying nearly 200 tanks, over 100 armoured personnel carriers and knocking out twelve Scud missiles, for no loss of their own.

The USAF stopped flying from Alconbury in 1995 and the runway area reverted to RAF control. This part of the airfield is now run by Urban and Civic Ltd and is being developed as an Enterprise Zone for businesses and about 5,000 houses. The development includes a heritage centre, to commemorate the history of the base. The remaining part of the site (the office blocks, facilities, military housing etc.) is still occupied by the USAF, but in 2015 the Pentagon announced that it would withdraw its personnel from Alconbury, probably by 2020.

RAF Wyton, one of Cambridgeshire's oldest airfields, is still fulfilling many different roles. In 1994 it ceased to be independent and was merged with nearby RAF Brampton. Wyton has now regained its status as an individual station, home of the Joint Forces Command, all operations having transferred over from Brampton.

One of the more well-known pilots based there in recent years was Rory Underwood, the England Rugby International. He scored forty-nine tries for England, making him one of the top scorers of all time. These days flying is limited to a training role, which is how it all began back in 1916.

Upwood was used by Bomber Command until the 1960s, then as a ground base for the RAF. In 1981, it was leased to the USAF as a satellite to Alconbury, but closed in 1994.

RAF Brampton has never been a flying station. Brampton Park was used by the Americans in the Second World War as an offshoot of their headquarters at Brampton Grange. It became RAF Brampton in 1955, the centre for RAF Support Command and the Joint Air Reconnaissance Intelligence Centre, which stayed there for fifty-seven years. In the 1990s, it was merged with RAF Wyton (RAF Henlow joined the group in 2001). In 2009 a review deemed Brampton surplus to requirements. The amalgamation was disbanded in 2012 and RAF Brampton became Brampton Camp. The Phantom aircraft that had guarded the gate was removed and the station closed at the end of 2013. The military buildings were demolished and at the time of writing the site was being redeveloped for housing.

Many former military sites have now been earmarked for huge new housing developments. One of the largest will be at Waterbeach Barracks, with a planning application for 6,500 houses in progress. Land at RAF Alconbury has been the subject of many schemes, including a new airport. Finally, permission was granted for the development of the old airfield as Alconbury Weald.

The new town of Northstowe is being built on the former RAF Oakington and surrounding farmland. Up to 10,000 new houses will be built to provide homes for 24,000 people (a town similar in size to Huntingdon). Around eight new schools will be built. The first primary school is already open with a secondary school due to open in 2019.

A further 420 houses are under way at RAF Brampton and 160 at RAF Upwood.

DUXFORD

After the end of the war, Duxford became home to Meteor jet fighters, for which the runway had to be extended. Ancillary buildings around the site became dilapidated, however, and rather than repair them, the RAF decided to move out. The last operational aircraft, a Meteor, took off in the summer of 1961 and for a few years that seemed to be end of the airfield.

But there was a surprising turn of events. In 1965, film producers Harry Saltzman and S. Benjamin Fisz decided they were going to make a big budget movie about the Battle of Britain. They tracked down, bought and borrowed as many Second World War-era aircraft as they could find, eventually ending up with over 100 aeroplanes, which, when brought together, made their fleet the 35th largest air force in the world at the time. During the summer of 1968 filming was carried out over the skies of Cambridgeshire, and the runways and hangars at Duxford once again echoed to the sound of Merlin engines.

The movie *The Battle of Britain* was released in 1969 and failed to make a profit, but the huge effort made to gather together so many historic aircraft gave enthusiasts the idea to create a museum. The East Anglian Aviation Society was soon set up at Duxford and kept a small but growing collection of old aircraft. The Imperial War Museum then started storing some of its own aircraft there. By the 1980s the airfield had become a popular visitor attraction, graced with a B-17 Flying Fortress *Sally B* and with the second British Concorde. In October 1983 an American B-52 bomber successfully landed at Duxford on the shortest runway a such an aircraft has ever landed on. It will never be able to take off again.

So, from almost facing oblivion, Duxford has probably now become the most famous Second World War airfield in the world. It is the most popular aviation museum in Europe. The American Air Museum was opened by the Queen in August 1997.

MOLESWORTH

The airfield at Molesworth reverted to RAF control in 1945 and was closed in 1946, but was reopened in 1951 for use by the US Air Force. It remains a US base today, home to the Joint Intelligence Operations Center Europe Analytic Center. In the 1970s it had been almost deserted, left unfenced and used by local people to learn to drive on the concrete roads.

All this changed in 1980, when Molesworth was one of two bases selected to hold US Ground Launched Cruise Missiles testing, a low-flying nuclear missile (the other being Greenham Common in Berkshire). A camp named Rainbow Fields Village was set up by a group of peace protesters next to the base. The group, named 'the smellies' by a national newspaper, were evicted but later returned to squat on 10 acres of land near the A1 at Brampton.

A second Peace Camp was set up in 1981, but there was little confrontation between protesters and military personnel until 1985, when the protesters were evicted. The 7-mile perimeter was fenced off in an operation involving 1,500 military personnel and police – the biggest military operation in England since the Second World War. The Campaign for Nuclear Disarmament (CND) staged a mass blockade a year later. Activists dressed as rabbits and teddy bears also drove into the base hidden in the back of a van and scaled an 80ft-high water tower. Security was not quite so tight in those days.

Most local residents were not supportive of the protesters and some reported being abused, to say nothing of the chaos caused on local roads. The local newspapers were certainly more concerned with the additional cost to the county of policing the area.

By 1987, CND were claiming that the missiles had arrived, but this was never confirmed, although they were already at Greenham Common, which became the target of much larger protests. The 303rd Tactical Missile Wing (a group linked to the famous 303rd Bomb Squadron based at Molesworth in the Second World War) had been activated on 12 December 1986. Shelters with 16ft ceilings made of alternate layers of concrete and earth had been constructed. They were capable of withstanding a direct hit by any known weapon.

In the event, only one flight (with sixteen missiles) ever became operational and the weapons were only at Molesworth for ten months. The deployment had led to talks between US President Ronald Reagan and USSR President Mikhail Gorbachev. A treaty curbing the use of Intermediate Nuclear Forces was signed in December 1987. By October 1988, the missiles had been flown out of Alconbury back to the USA for destruction. A party of Russian inspectors visited the site soon after to make sure that all the missiles had gone. Molesworth's involvement with nuclear weapons was at an end.

Molesworth is still in use these days as an intelligence centre, and the US European and African Command Joint Analysis Centre and NATO Intelligence Fusion Centre are based there. In 2015, however, the Ministry of Defence announced that US activity at Molesworth would come to an end.

7

ROYAL CAMBRIDGESHIRE

Medieval monarchs were frequent visitors to the great monasteries at Ely and elsewhere in Cambridgeshire. **Henry II,** however, visited Huntingdon in 1174 for a different reason: to lay siege to the rebel William the Lion of Scotland (also titled the Earl of Huntingdon) who was holed up in Huntingdon Castle. The King, fresh from doing penance for the murder of Thomas Becket, was successful in crushing the rebels and Huntingdon's castle was burned to the ground.

VIEW of CAMBRIDGE CASTLE.

Queen Elizabeth I set the tone for later royal visits to Cambridge in 1564 when she stayed at the Provost's Lodge at King's College. Elizabeth travelled in style, bringing her whole entourage with her. Her Secretary, William Cecil, stayed at St John's, his old college, while Sir Robert Dudley, the Queen's favourite, stayed at Trinity, the Maids of Honour at Gonville and Caius, and the household officials at Queens'.

The Queen was entertained by great debates and progressed around all the colleges except Jesus College, which was 'too remote'. Things didn't go quite as well as planned, however, as the churchwardens of Great St Mary's were fined 2*s* 2*d* for not ringing the bells when the Queen arrived.

Queen Elizabeth travelled on to Huntingdon, where she stayed with the Cromwells at Hinchingbrooke House. **James I** was also entertained there on his journey south from Scotland to take the English throne in 1603.

Subsequent royal visitors to Cambridge stayed at Trinity College. James I enjoyed his entertainment there so much in March 1615 that he returned again in May to see a re-run of the play *The Ignoramus*. It perhaps shows how little things might have changed for university students that the Vice Chancellor ordered that 'no Graduate, scholar or student of this university presume to resort to any Inn, Tavern, Alehouse or Tobacco shop at any time during the abode of His Majesty here.'

King James visited again in 1623 and 1624. He had a tendency to return time and time again to stay at places he liked, especially if there was good hunting to be had nearby. This was an honour to his hosts if they could afford it, but the Cromwell family at Hinchingbrooke House was ruined by the expense of James' visits and finally they had to sell up and move to Ramsey.

Student behaviour obviously hadn't improved by the time James' son **Charles I** arrived with his queen, Henrietta Maria, in 1632. The students again had to be ordered to be on their best behaviour and that 'no rude or immodest exclamations be made, no humming, hawking, whistling, hissing or laughing or any stamping or knocking, nor any other such uncivil or unscholarlike or boyish demeanour upon any occasion'.

Thirteen years later things had fallen apart for Charles I and he was attacking the town of Huntingdon with his troops, just one skirmish in his Civil War with the forces of Parliament. When in 1647 Charles returned to Cambridgeshire again he was now a captive, held at Childerley Hall a few miles west of Cambridge.

Later monarchs visited Cambridge on the way to or from Newmarket, where they enjoyed the horse racing and hunting.

William Prince of Orange visited briefly whilst in England in 1670. Who knew then that he would be returning to Cambridge as **King William III** of England in 1689? His sister-in-law Queen Anne visited in 1705 when she knighted Isaac Newton, Professor of Mathematics and Fellow of Trinity College.

The cost of this hospitality was huge and the feasts spectacular. Even William's Yeoman of the Guard consumed thirty-seven bottles of wine while they were staying at the Red Lion.

DINNER GIVEN to 15,000 Persons on PARKER'S PIECE, CAMBRIDGE in the presence of 25,000 Spectators *Thursday 28th June 1838*

Huge crowds greeted **Queen Victoria and Prince Albert** when they made their first royal visit to Cambridge in 1843. The Queen was rather bored by the Latin speeches but enjoyed a visit to the Geological Museum, where she and the Prince were shown round by Adam Sedgwick.

Victoria and Albert returned to Cambridge in 1847, this time travelling on the train, just two years after the railway line was opened. Prince Albert was installed as Chancellor of the University.

Cambridge's most frequent royal visitor was **George V**. He first arrived in 1912 to inspect the large-scale army manoeuvres being held in the Gog Magog hills area. Attitudes towards royalty were changing and George was not quite as universally welcomed as his predecessors. During a 1914 visit a group of Suffragettes threw leaflets at the royal car. The King's later visits during the First World War were devoted to inspecting the troops and the casualties in the First Eastern General Hospital in Cambridge rather than feasting at the University. Soon after war was declared, he visited Huntingdon to inspect the troops of the Highland Mounted Brigade on Portholme Meadow.

After the war George V's visits returned to normal, including opening the new Cambridge University Library in 1934, which was built on the site of the First Eastern General Hospital that he had previously visited.

George's wife, Queen Mary, was much more interested in Stanley Woolston's antique shop in Emmanuel Street and made numerous visits there, sometimes bringing her daughter-in-law Elizabeth and granddaughter Princess Margaret. Among other things she purchased tiny ivory objects for her famous dolls' house. On one such visit, the royal car broke down and she was given a lift from Waterbeach to Cambridge by local man Percy Titmous.

George VI and **Queen Elizabeth** had good reason to enjoy their visits to Cambridge. George VI, a former Trinity student, returned to his old college in 1947 to join in the 400th anniversary celebrations and recalled his happy days there as an undergraduate. A year later Queen Elizabeth became the first woman to receive a degree from Cambridge University in a ceremony at Senate House.

George VI and Queen Elizabeth also made several trips to the local area during the Second World War to help keep up morale. They visited airbases such as Warboys and Witchford, and travelled to Burwell Fen, where they talked to women serving with the Land Army.

Amazingly, it was not until 1955 that a reigning sovereign visited the Mayor and Corporation of Cambridge at the Guildhall. **Queen Elizabeth II** and **Prince Philip** acknowledged the crowds in the Market Square from the balcony before leaving to open the new School of Veterinary Medicine in Madingley Road. The Queen returned to Cambridgeshire in 1973 when she visited the King's School in Ely for its centenary celebrations.

Two years later, on her first visit to Peterborough as a reigning monarch, Queen Elizabeth distributed the Maundy Money to forty-nine men and women in the Cathedral. (She would later distribute the Maundy Money to sixty-one men and women at Ely in 1987.) In 1978 she was back in Peterborough to officially open the new Magistrates' Court and the Cresset complex at Bretton, as well as visiting the National Shire Horse Society centenary show at Alwalton. Ten years after this visit the Queen returned to Peterborough for the 750th Anniversary celebrations at Peterborough Cathedral. As usual with her busy schedule, the Queen also opened the Edith Cavell Hospital and the Norwich and Peterborough HQ in Lynch Wood. Interestingly, Lorraine Cherry from Werrington presented the Queen with a bouquet in both 1978 and 1988. The Queen's last visit to the area was in 1991.

There were more centenary celebrations for the Queen to attend in November 2009. On 19 November the Queen and Prince Philip arrived at Ely by train to celebrate the Cathedral's 900th anniversary, after which they travelled to Cambridge in the afternoon to mark the 800th anniversary of the foundation of Cambridge University and the 100th anniversary of the establishment of Marshall Aerospace.

The Queen returned to Cambridge in 2013. Like Queen Victoria before her, she travelled on a newly opened form of public transport – this time the Cambridgeshire Guided Busway – during a visit to the Addenbrooke's Medical Campus to open the new Rosie Maternity Hospital.

The Duke of Edinburgh has visited Cambridge many times. Like Prince Albert, Prince Philip was installed as Chancellor of the University, in June 1977. He has visited the University on numerous occasions since then to carry out his duties.

Other royal visitors to the city over the years include **King Christian VII** of Denmark and Norway in 1768; **Louis XVIII** of France in 1812 (he was in exile at the time); **Pedro II** Emperor of Brazil in 1871; and **Aga Khan III** in 1914. When Crown Prince (later to be Emperor) Hirohito of Japan arrived in 1921, it was the first time the heir to the Japanese throne had been allowed out of the country. He visited the Leys School, where several prominent Japanese had been educated. On the same visit he also went to Ely Cathedral, watched students rowing on the River Cam and dined with Nobel Prize-winning physicist J.J. Thomson.

Tafari Makonnen was awarded an Honorary Doctorate of Law at Cambridge in 1924. Six years later in Addis Ababa, he was proclaimed **Emperor Haile Selassie** of Ethiopia. He returned to England following Italy's invasion of the country and, from 1936 to 1941, lived in Bath, before returning to his homeland to fight the invaders. Another member of foreign royalty to visit Cambridge was **King Peter II**, the last ever King of Yugoslavia. He was the first student to study at the University while at the same time being a monarch, although he was in exile at the time, having left Yugoslavia in 1941 when the Germans invaded. He never regained his throne and died in Colorado in 1970.

Of course, many notable foreign students who studied at Cambridge University have gone on to great things. No fewer than three Indian Prime Ministers, Jawaharlal Nehru, Rajiv Ghandi and Dr Manmohan Singh, all studied there. Dina bint Abdul-Hamid, an English literature undergraduate at Girton College and later lecturer of English literature at Cairo University, went on to marry King Hussein of Jordan in 1955. There are many more examples.

Several royals have carried the title Earl and latterly Duke of Cambridge, most recently, of course, Prince William, second in line to the British throne. The Earldom of Huntingdon has at times been associated with the royal house of Scotland, notably King David I.

8

DISASTERS

THE ABBOTS RIPTON RAILWAY DISASTER

In 1876 a train crash occurred near Huntingdon, which was to have unexpected consequences for the town. The accident happened during a snowstorm on 21 January, when the Special Scotch Express, later renamed the Flying Scotsman, travelling from Edinburgh to London reached Abbots Ripton travelling at full speed, around 45mph. It crashed into a coal train that was being shunted into sidings. The train derailed, pulling its carriages onto the northbound line.

The accident was caused by the snowstorm affecting the old-fashioned semaphore-style signals, which were weighed down by snow. The problem was exacerbated by the custom in those days of leaving signals at 'clear'. The signal levers had been put to 'danger' to stop the express until the goods train was off the main line, but the weight of snow meant that the signals themselves could not change to indicate the danger.

The guard of the Scotch Express ran towards Peterborough with a red lamp and succeeded in stopping the next southbound train, while the fireman of the coal train placed warning detonators (used as signals in fog) on the tracks northbound from Huntingdon, but there was not enough time to prevent tragedy. A northbound London to Leeds and York express sped past more jammed signals and its driver did not realise anything was wrong until he set off the warning detonators. By this time it was too late. He slammed his engine into reverse but there was no time for this to take effect before his train ploughed into the carriages of the Scotch Express. Thirteen people were killed and sixty-nine more were injured.

One of those killed in the disaster was the eldest son of actor and playwright Dion Boucicault, also called Dion but known as Willie. He was buried in Huntingdon cemetery. In recognition of the kindness and respect the people of Huntingdon had shown his family, Dion Boucicault offered to provide the town with a drinking fountain or legacy to provide income for the poor. The Town Council had other ideas, however, and after several exchanges of letters they persuaded Boucicault to fund the restoration of the old Grammar School buildings to the tune of £900. Huntingdon architect Robert Hutchinson drew up plans

which included a stone figure on the west end of the roof facing Market Square and a bell tower at the other end. The classroom would also be extended by 16ft.

The building had been encased in red brick since Elizabethan times. When this façade wall at the Market Square end was removed, it was found to be covering a finely decorated Norman arch. It was also discovered that the level of the High Street had risen considerably over time and the base of the wall was far below the level of the modern street. So the whole Grammar School building was dismantled in 1877 with the utmost care, each piece being numbered. It was then painstakingly rebuilt stone by stone on a new foundation, the entire building being raised by 3 or 4ft above its former level. The building now houses the Cromwell Museum.

THE FEN DITTON FERRY DISASTER

On the afternoon of 10 June 1905 three young women were drowned at Fen Ditton when the *Plough Ferry* capsized in the middle of the river. It was the day of the May Bumps rowing races, which had attracted huge crowds of spectators. When the rowing finished, hordes of people wanted to cross the river using the flat-bottomed *Grind Ferry*, which was pulled across by a chain. On the third trip about twenty people were crammed into the boat, when two more men leapt on just as it pulled away. The ferry began to take on water and people surged to one side to try and stop the water coming in; this caused the whole boat to tip over and everyone fell into the river. The tragedy took place in full view of hundreds of people and several young men dived in and rescued as many as they could. Unfortunately, three women, wearing long cumbersome skirts, got entangled in the railing attached to the side of the ferry and were dragged under water. Minnie Murkin, Violet Handscombe and Annie Thompson all died. Tragically, Minnie was due to be married that very day and had been watching the festivities with her fiancé, who had crossed the river on the previous ferry. The inquest heard that the ferrymen may have been drunk, but the verdict was accidental death.

THE SOMERSHAM AIR CRASH

On Monday, 5 October 1942 a Wellington bomber of 156 Pathfinder squadron took off from RAF Warboys on its way to Germany. It had only flown a few miles when a flare ignited on board and set fire to the aircraft. The crew all bailed out safely, but the stricken aircraft took the roof off a house in Rectory Lane as it descended before crashing into cottages adjoining the White Lion pub in Somersham, where it exploded. Seven houses were wrecked by the crash or gutted by the huge fire that followed. Firemen, Home Guard members, civil defence, soldiers and airmen from St Ives, Ramsey and Huntingdon all fought heroically to extinguish the blaze. Mobile canteens from Huntingdon and Chatteris served hot drinks, soup and sandwiches for the firefighters throughout the night.

The crash killed eleven civilians, ranging in age from Pauline Catterick, who was just 11 months old, to Annie Mary Holditch, aged 74. The other victims on the night were Eliza Nightingale, Violet Maude, Vera Catterick, Alice and Frank Lamb, Elsie Taylor, Elizabeth Richardson and Ena Stroud. The eleventh victim, 4-year-old Juliana Davies, died in hospital on the following Wednesday. At the funeral an RAF lorry covered in flowers carried all eleven victims through the streets of Somersham, which were lined by the entire population of the village. An RAF plane circled overhead and dipped one wing in salute. Sir Arthur 'Bomber' Harris himself visited RAF Wyton on 9 October to give the crews encouragement after this tragic incident.

MORE SECOND WORLD WAR DISASTERS

The Somersham crash of 1942 was sadly not the only aircraft incident of the Second World War. Indeed, as the war went on the greatest danger to Cambridgeshire and Huntingdonshire's residents came not from the Luftwaffe but from RAF and US Army Air Force accidents. Air-raid documents kept by Huntingdonshire County Council, for instance, show that there were at least eleven major crashes in the county during the two-year period from March 1943 to April 1945, either from damaged aeroplanes limping back to base after a raid or, far more dangerously, aircraft fully loaded with bombs exploding on take-off.

On the night of Saturday, 6 November 1943, two Wellington bombers, taking part in a night flying exercise, collided over Huntingdon. One came down near Abbots Ripton, the second just yards from the Officers' Mess at Brampton Park. Captain Clay Snedegar, an intelligence officer based at Brampton Grange, was first on the scene at Brampton:

> There was a terrific explosion, sending flames 100–150 ft high. Machine gun ammunition was exploding in all directions from the heat. It was dark and the billowing flames lit up the sky like daylight... One of the bodies pulled from the wreckage was that of a young woman. She was a brown-haired girl and the flames from the wreckage lit up the golden tones in her hair... For nearly a hundred yards in all directions, bits of plane, grass and trees were burning fiercely... At the base of a very large tree was the body of the fifth crew member. He was lying face down with his head jammed against the base of the tree... The impact had knocked off his flying boots: they were 2 or 3 ft from his body.

Only the pilots from each plane survived.

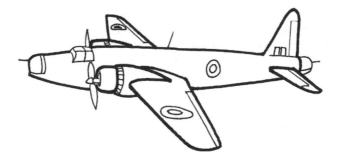

THE SOHAM RAILWAY EXPLOSION

At the beginning of June 1944 vast amounts of munitions were being shipped across Britain as part of the build-up for D-Day. In the early hours of Friday 2 June, a train pulling forty-five wagons and carrying about 400 tons of high-explosive bombs was steaming very carefully and slowly (about 15mph) along the March to Soham line when the driver, Benjamin Gimbert, looked back and saw that the wagon immediately behind his tender was burning. He slowly stopped the train – it took about three minutes to do that, as any jolt could have been disastrous – and his fireman Jim Nightall uncoupled the rest of the wagons. Gimbert then started the locomotive moving again with its one burning wagon, in the hope of getting it through Soham station and into the open fens beyond, where it could destroy itself without harm to anyone, but the wagon, with 5 tons of high explosive on board, exploded as it passed through the station. Gimbert was thrown into the air and landed on the ground outside the Station Hotel, but the fireman Jim Nightall and station signalman Frank Bridges were both killed. The fire then spread to some nearby gas holders. Many people ran to the scene to douse the flames and save the injured, including the local Home Guard and ARP wardens, the Fire Service, the Women's Voluntary Service, local Rescue and Ambulance Parties and officers from nearby RAF bases.

Sunrise revealed a scene of utter devastation. Where the station had been was now a crater 15ft deep. The shop windows in Soham had been blown to pieces and the locomotive itself, a very heavy 2-8-0 Austerity type, had been thrown clean off the rails. Nearly 800 properties had been damaged, thirteen of them beyond repair. The railway line was wrecked, but it was still needed for the transport of weapons for D-Day, so repairs were carried out immediately. At five o'clock in the morning, just over three hours after the explosion, the locomotive was re-railed back onto the tracks and taken away. A group of engineers from the US Army arrived later that morning to fill in the crater and to lay new tracks. Astonishingly, the line was reopened for traffic by 8.20 p.m. on the same day as the explosion.

Benjamin Gimbert and, posthumously, Jim Nightall were both awarded the George Cross for their actions in saving Soham from an even greater disaster, for if the entire train had exploded then the whole town would have been wiped off the map. The cause of the explosion was never properly ascertained. It could have been an overheating axle, a spark from the engine or from one going past, or it could even perhaps have been sabotage.

Engine driver Benjamin Gimbert lived until 1978. Small pieces of shrapnel slowly emerged from his body for the rest of his life. In 1994, to commemorate the fiftieth anniversary of the explosion, students at Soham Village College made a new town sign that incorporated a railway locomotive against a background of flames and Anthony Day published a gripping account of the disaster, *But for Men Such as These: The Heroes of the Railway Incident at Soham, Cambridgeshire in June 1944.*

THE GREAT FLOODS

The gales of the cold winter of 1946/47 were the worst in living memory in the Fens. The winds had driven huge snowfalls into immense drifts up to 6ft high. In March, as the thaw took hold, all the rivers rose alarmingly as the snow melted while yet more rain came down. The river banks could not cope with the immense pressure of water and one night the banks gave way in some places and were overtopped in others. More and more water surged across the Fens, flooding houses right up to the ceilings and forcing people to evacuate their homes through upstairs windows. More than 600 families had to evacuate their properties on a single day. The army and POWs (there were still some from the war) were brought in to plug breaches wherever they could, but once a bank has been breached there is often little that can be done in reality until the flood levels start to subside naturally. So much flood water soaked into the ground that the foundations of many buildings were compromised, causing the properties to collapse. Many crops stayed submerged into the summer. The ultimate cost of the damage was calculated at £13 million (roughly £500 million at today's prices). A further £7 million was spent afterwards to create a new relief river on the eastern side of the Fens.

It was probably the worst Fenland flood in four centuries and there was much discussion at the time as to why the flood should have been so devastating in an area that was already richly provided with pumping machinery, sluices and catchment drains. Fenland historian Trevor Bevis, who saw the floods of 1947 first-hand, suggests that all this artificial protection may itself have been part of the problem, because it encouraged people to become complacent about the power of water. In the Middle Ages, on the other hand, the people of the Fens knew all about floods and were, to some extent, prepared for them.

THE THORNEY TOLL AIR CRASH

On 28 August 1976 a huge C-114 Starlifter cargo jet belonging to the United States Air Force was on its way back to RAF Mildenhall from America when it encountered a violent thunderstorm and heavy rains over Thorney. The aircraft was hit by lightning and it seems to have broken up in mid-air.

Witnesses to the crash reported seeing pieces of the aircraft fall to the ground across a wide area. Ian Simmons was taking his boat down river from Peterborough to Wisbech that evening and was near Thorney Toll when he saw 'a fireball rising up from behind the north bank. It looked like the rising sun at first then mushroomed into an orange ball of fire. Initially I thought that the lightning had perhaps struck a fuel storage tank but then I saw another smaller fireball dropping from the sky.' Parts of the Starlifter were scattered across the fields around Thorney Toll, with one engine found half a mile from the main crash site. By the time the volunteers of Thorney's fire brigade arrived at the scene the place was an inferno and it took seven appliances 26 hours to extinguish the fires.

Fourteen American crew members and four passengers were killed on the flight. There were no survivors. A memorial to the tragedy is situated close to the crash site, near the end of the Thorney Dyke road.

THE HUNTINGDON AIR CRASH

During the 1970s the RAF regularly flew large aircraft from the airfield at Wyton, despite complaints from residents of Huntingdon, who frequently called for the flights to be stopped. On 3 May 1977 a Canberra was returning from a two-hour reconnaissance flight over Scotland, flown by Flight Lieutenant John Armitage and Flight Lieutenant Lawrence Davies. The aircraft was clearly in trouble as it flew low over the town. Huntingdon resident Keith Sisman told the *Daily Express*, 'the pilot was obviously trying to get away from the houses. He must have known he was finished, but he tried to save the school and the estate.'

The Canberra missed Sapley Park School, where 245 children were about to go home for lunch, but its wing hit a row of houses in Norfolk Road and blazing fuel spilled out in a ball of fire. Tracey Middleton, aged 4, and her 2-year-old sister Kelly were among those who died, along with 4-month-old Adrian Thompson. Six other people were injured and seven houses were completely destroyed. Mr Evans from Sycamore Drive said 'it was absolutely terrifying. It looked as if a giant bomb had hit the whole place. There were women crying in the street.'

The Mayor of Huntingdon launched an appeal for £25,000 for the families who had lost their children and homes, and a planned Silver Jubilee parade through Huntingdon by the officers of RAF Wyton was cancelled. In November 1977, the Secretary of State reported to Parliament on the cause of the crash. The Canberra had been practising a manoeuvre called an 'overshoot on asymmetric power', which simulated a landing in which one of the aircraft's two engines had failed. The pilot had started the manoeuvre correctly, descending in a right-hand turn with one engine throttled back. He was then supposed to level the wings and head for the runway, but instead the aircraft's angle of bank increased as the wing dipped down further, which led into a downward spiral and a near-vertical crash into the ground. The RAF's inquiry concluded that the crash was therefore pilot error because he had not levelled the wings and he had throttled too much power into the other engine. The inquest jury returned verdicts of accidental death on all five people who died.

In March 1991 another Canberra bomber from RAF Wyton crashed, this time on take-off. The aircraft came down on the busy Huntingdon–March A141, killing its crew of three, but no cars were hit.

THE SOHAM FIRE

In July 1846, a huge fire ripped through Hall Street in Soham. It was started by arsonists at about half past one in the morning. Fortunately, the glow of the fire was spotted and soon fifteen families, eighty-two people in all, had been evacuated from their homes. The fire destroyed eight houses, four large barns and killed much livestock, although fortunately no people were harmed.

The most impressive spectacle was the burning of a five-storey-high windmill. The *Cambridge Independent Press* for 11 July 1846 described it in detail:

> The scene now was truly magnificent, though exceedingly awful; a huge body of smoke ascended from the houses, towards the mill, the sails of which caught fire, and the smoke being converted to flames, and the sails turning in the wind, gave one of the grandest scenes that can possibly be imagined. In fact, the most accomplished pyrotechnist could not have produced an effect so grand, though he had called his best artistic skill to his aid, especially when the exterior of the mill was destroyed, and the fantastic works were displayed, glowing with red and white heat, the sails yet whirling in the air.

THE CHATTERIS FIRE

Chatteris seems prone to fires. In 1310, a large fire spread through the town, almost completely destroying the nunnery and severely damaging the church, which is why nothing at the church dates from earlier than the mid-fourteenth century. A later fire in 1706 destroyed many of the town's medieval buildings.

On the morning of Wednesday, 14 September 1864, an arsonist set fire to a stack of wheat at Hive End. That summer had been a very dry one, so the fields and thatched roofs of houses were vulnerable to even the slightest spark. The fire soon spread through the town, causing over £10,000 worth of damage (equivalent to £11 million today); it destroyed more than 100 houses and killed a 7-year-old girl. A relief fund of £300 (worth about £35,000 today) was raised for the victims.

9

BRICKS AND MORTAR: THE BUILDINGS OF CAMBRIDGESHIRE

Cambridge is best known, of course, for its iconic university and college buildings such as King's College Chapel, Trinity's Wren Library and the Mathematical Bridge at Queens', but there is much more to the county than this.

CATHEDRALS

Almost 100 religious houses existed in Cambridgeshire at one time or another before the Dissolution of the Monasteries. Some were large and important, none more so than the great **Benedictine Abbey at Ramsey**, noted in the Fens for both its wealth and its learning. In its heyday it was home to around eighty monks and had an impressive library, some of which still survives. The Abbey was known as 'Ramsey the Golden' on account of its vast wealth.

After the Reformation, most religious establishments were sold off for private houses or left empty and their stone looted for local buildings. The Abbey at Ramsey was granted to Sir Richard Williams, nephew of the architect of the Dissolution of the Monasteries, Thomas Cromwell. Ramsey's medieval gateway was transported to the Williams/Cromwell's other house at Hinchingbrooke in Huntingdon. A large house was constructed on the site as a summer residence by Richard's son Henry, who now called himself Cromwell. This later became the family's main residence when they ran out of money and had to sell Hinchingbrooke.

The Abbey's infirmary survives today as the parish church of St Thomas à Becket, and stone from another part of the Abbey was used to build the church tower, as well as the tower of Holywell church. Within 200 years, almost all the Abbey's stone had disappeared, much of it taken away to Cambridge for the construction of several colleges including Gonville and Caius. The gatehouse (without the lost gateway) still remains and is cared for by the National Trust.

The abbeys at Ely and Peterborough were luckier in that they were not handed over to private families but were instead refounded as cathedrals. **Ely Cathedral**, which can be seen for miles around, is known as the 'ship of the fens'. It is the third longest cathedral in England at 537ft long (161m) and has dominated the landscape for 900 years. It was once part of an abbey founded in AD 673 by Etheldreda, daughter of the East Anglian King Anna. Ely attracted many gifts of land from benefactors such as Brithnoth, Earl of Essex, and grew rich despite its remote position in the (then) undrained Fens. Work on the current building began soon after the Norman Conquest. The building stone was brought in by water, mainly from the quarries at Barnack. The Norman tower collapsed in 1322 with such force that it shook the whole area like an earthquake. Work on the new octagonal lantern tower and Lady Chapel took twenty years and cost £2,000, which by some measures would be the equivalent of £615 million today. The Cathedral was closed during the Civil War and its Bishop, Matthew Wren, was imprisoned in the Tower of London for eighteen years. He was only released on the restoration of Charles II.

Many of the original monastic buildings survive at Ely. Most are now part of the King's School, such as the Queen's House, which has become the headmaster's house. The former Bishop's Palace became a Red Cross hospital in the Second World War, then a Sue Ryder Home. This too has been taken over and is now the sixth form centre of the King's School. The national Stained Glass Museum opened in the triforium of the Cathedral in 1979. It receives around 250,000 visitors every year and the Cathedral costs £6,000 a day to run.

Peterborough Cathedral has seen some famous visitors. King Stephen, King Henry II (with Thomas Becket), King John, King Henry III and Kings Edward I, Edward II and Edward III all visited or stayed here. Both King Henry VI and Henry VII visited Peterborough. In between times, the town and Abbey had been sacked by the Lancastrian army of Henry VI's queen, Margaret of Anjou, so the King may not have been warmly welcomed. In 1646, during the Civil War, Charles I was imprisoned here for two nights by the Parliamentarians.

Peterborough was the site of the first recorded monastery in Cambridgeshire. Then called Medeswell or Medeshamstede, it was first mentioned in AD 655. It was a Benedictine foundation dedicated to Saints Peter, Paul and Andrew. Its location meant that it was vulnerable to attack from the Danes, so a small castle was built nearby to defend it, the remains of which can still be seen today. The monastery was also attacked by Hereward the Wake in 1070. By this time, the town, which had grown up around the Abbey, was becoming known as the Burgh of St Peter or Peterborough. The Abbey was destroyed again, by fire, in 1116. Although the buildings were rebuilt and the Abbey became reasonably prosperous again, it was badly hit by the Black Death and never fully recovered.

The most precious relic of the medieval Abbey was the arm of St Oswald, which had been stolen by one of the monks from Bamburgh Castle. The arm was then lost around the time of the Reformation. The Abbey itself was spared by Henry VIII, who decreed that its church should become a cathedral and installed a bishop (the former abbot) to tighten his grip on the Church in the area.

Two queens were buried in Peterborough Cathedral during the Tudor period. Catherine of Aragon's tomb is in the north aisle near the High Altar, while Mary Queen of Scots was buried on the opposite side of the altar, following her execution at Fortheringhay in Northamptonshire. Her grave is now empty as she was re-buried in Westminster in 1612 by her son James, who was then King of England as well as Scotland.

Henry VIII also founded a grammar school in the grounds of the former abbey, which became known as the King's School. A girls' school was founded in 1870 and remained open until 1928. Edith Cavell attended the school as a pupil/teacher. The boys' school moved from the precincts to Park Road in 1885; most of the monastic stone was carried away and used to build Thorpe Hall.

Peterborough Cathedral suffered badly during the English Civil War. The town had Royalist sympathies and so was attacked by Oliver Cromwell. His troops smashed most of the stained glass and demolished the altar, reredos and Lady Chapel. Much of Peterborough's library was burnt in the cloisters. The original wooden ceiling survives in the nave, however; the only one of its period in the country and one of only four in Europe.

MORE RELIGIOUS HOUSES

Almost every town or village across the county had some sort of religious house or establishment before the Reformation, although many were small operations by that time. Most had been set up by wealthy benefactors who were able to give a grant of land. These religious houses were often used as retirement homes for widows or as places to send unmarried daughters or younger sons so they didn't upset the stability of the family. In consequence, many residents were not motivated by religious devotion. Families would make large grants of money to ensure they lived in comfort. Some of these religious institutions survive as churches, such as Thorney Abbey Church, while others like Sawtry Abbey have disappeared completely. Other former religious houses survive in different ways. The Benedictine Nunnery of St Radegund in Cambridge was refounded as Jesus College. The Priory at Barnwell is remembered in the area now by the name of the Cambridge United football ground – the Abbey Stadium.

THORNEY ABBEY, *in* CAMBRIDGESHIRE.

Published according to Act of Parliament by Jno. Hogg Nth Paternoster Row .

Another religious institution that met its end at the Dissolution was the Hospital of St John the Baptist in Huntingdon, a twelfth-century foundation set up to care for travellers passing through the town. The Hospital ceased operating around 1547, whereupon the buildings remained unoccupied until Sir Anthony Bartelmewe decided to set up a school there for the sons of burgesses. Most of the old Hospital's buildings were pulled down but some of the infirmary hall was converted into a two-storey school, with the classroom on the ground floor and the headmaster's lodgings on the upper floor. The building continued to be used as part of Huntingdon Grammar School until the Second World War. Since 1962, it has been the home of the **Cromwell Museum** and has on display an unrivalled collection of Cromwelliana.

A particularly rare survival is **Chesterton Tower** near Cambridge. In 1217 Henry III presented the Papal legate, Cardinal Guala of Vercelli near Milan in Italy, with the church and living of Chesterton. The Cardinal in turn donated Chesterton to Vercelli Abbey. In the middle of the fourteenth century the Abbey arranged for a two-storey house to be constructed for the 'procurator', who was their representative on the ground at Chesterton. It looks today like it was once part of a much larger building but it is, in fact, an entirely self-contained residence. In 1440, Henry VI took the property back and gave it to King's Hall, which would later become part of Trinity College.

BISHOPS ON THE MOVE

There are three former Bishops' Palaces in Cambridgeshire. The Bishop of Ely had his first stopping point on his journey to London at **Somersham**, to which he could travel by water. He had a second residence at **Wisbech**, built on the site of the castle by Bishop, later Cardinal, Morton. The Bishop of Lincoln had his palace at **Buckden** on the Great North Road. It was used by many important visitors. Henry VIII's two nephews were there when they died in 1531 and Catherine of Aragon was held there, too.

The buildings have suffered very different fortunes. Buckden Palace still remains and is the home of an order of Clarentian Missionaries, but Morton's Palace was replaced by a mansion house in the seventeenth century, while at Somersham, only a single fragment of the walls survives.

CHURCHES

The oldest surviving building in Cambridgeshire is **St Bene't's Church** in Cambridge. The tower dates from around 1020 in the reign of King Canute, and was probably built to contain the bells, although the earliest mention of bells at St Bene't's dates only from the thirteenth century, when the bells were used to summon students to lectures and examinations. St Bene't's is located in the road of the same name, just off King's Parade in Cambridge. Its other claim to fame is that it is thought that the art of 'change ringing' (ringing a set of church bells to a set pattern) originated here.

S. BENEDICT'S.

The Holy Sepulchre or Round Church, Cambridge.

Another ecclesiastical building of note in the city is the **Church of the Holy Sepulchre,** more popularly known as the Round Church, which is one of only four round churches in England. It was built around 1130 on land donated by the Abbot of Ramsey, and it is probably associated with the Knights Templar, who built similar churches elsewhere. It originally had a taller bell tower, but this was replaced in the mid-nineteenth century. Cambridgeshire has two round tower churches, at Snailwell and Bartlow.

Another early ecclesiastical building is Cambridge's **Leper Chapel** on Newmarket Road. This fine Norman survival was once the chapel of the Hospital of St Mary Magdelene, which owned Stourbridge Fair. By the nineteenth century it was used only as a stable but the Victorians recognised the building's importance and Sir George Gilbert Scott carried out extensive restoration work.

St Wendreda's Church at March is known for its magnificent double hammer beam angel roof. There are approximately 120 angels carved on the roof and it is thought by experts to be one of the finest examples of its kind. If you look closely between the first and second windows on the south side you will see that the medieval craftsmen carved a devil amongst the angels.

The **Church of the Scared Heart** in St Ives is probably the only one to have been moved piece by piece to a new location. It was designed by the famous church architect Augustus Pugin and was originally built in Cambridge in 1841 as the Church of St Andrew. At that time, it had been the first Roman Catholic church built in Cambridgeshire since the Reformation. By 1902 it had been superseded by the new Church of Our Lady and the English Martyrs in Cambridge. A St Ives businessman, George Pauling, purchased the church for £1,000 and had it moved to St Ives. It was dismantled and transported by barge, and rebuilt within five months.

The **Church of Our Lady and the English Martyrs**, situated at the junction of Hills Road and Lensfield Road, also has interesting origins. It was financed by a former Parisian ballerina, known as 'the beauty of her age', Yolande Duvernay. She had married Stephens Lyne-Stephens, reputedly the richest commoner in England. Despite their wealth, the couple were not really accepted in the highest society due to Yolande's past liaisons – she had been sold for sex by her mother since the age of 15. As a widow, Yolande was said to have more money than Queen Victoria. She used much of it for charity, including building several churches, the most impressive of which was the Church of Our Lady and the English Martyrs in Cambridge.

CASTLES

You may not realise it now, but Cambridgeshire once had several castles. Some, like Eaton Socon (originally in Bedfordshire) and Castle Camps, may have been in existence in Saxon times. Several, such as Cambridge Castle, Huntingdon Castle and Aldreth Castle, were built on the orders of William the Conqueror, to defend against Hereward the Wake; nothing remains of Aldreth Castle now and no one is even certain where it was.

Others, like Burwell Castle and Wood Walton Castle, were built during the troubled reign of King Stephen in the early twelfth century to defend against the powerful rebel Geoffrey de Mandeville, Earl of Essex. Mandeville besieged Burwell and received a mortal wound from a crossbow bolt. Many more 'castles' were little more than fortified manor houses, such as those at Bassingbourn, Bourn and Elton Hall.

One of the best examples of these later castles is **Kimbolton Castle**. Although there was a wooden motte and bailey castle built in Norman times at Kimbolton, it was not on the site of the current castle. All that remains of it is a low mound, surrounded by a ditch. When Kimbolton was granted a charter to hold a market by King John, the town was redesigned and a large market area was created along the High Street in the centre, with the church at one end and a new castle at the other. This castle was probably a fortified house, although none of the original buildings survive. By the 1520s, it had been rebuilt as a Tudor manor house and was owned by the Wingfield family. It was chosen as the residence for Queen Catherine of Aragon, who had been divorced by King Henry VIII and replaced by Anne Boleyn. The Queen was held here as a semi-prisoner from 1534 until her death in 1536 and her ghost is reputed to haunt the castle.

Another resident of Kimbolton Castle was Sir John Popham. During his early life he was said to have been a highwayman, but he became a Lord Chief Justice and is best known for presiding at the trial of Guy Fawkes in 1605. In 1615 the castle passed to the Montagu family, who became Earls and then Dukes of Manchester. During the Second World War the house was used by the Royal Army Medical Corps. By 1950 the family's money was running out and the estate was sold to Kimbolton School.

The current building dates from the period 1690–1720, when it was almost entirely rebuilt by two of the period's most fashionable architects, Sir John Vanbrugh and Nicholas Hawksmoor. Battlements were included to keep the castle feel. There are many fine interior wall paintings by Antonio Pellegrini dating from this period, too. Another top name, Robert Adam, was responsible for the gatehouse, built in the 1760s.

Very little now remains of most of Cambridgeshire's castles. At **Kirtling**, the tower is a remnant of the manor house Kirtling Hall, rather than the castle that pre-dated it. It is said that in 1260 three men were carrying a cask of wine across the bridge (probably a drawbridge) when it collapsed under their weight, so perhaps the whole building was suspect. The mansion that replaced it, belonging to the North family, was built in the 1530s and was demolished in 1801. Only its three-storey gatehouse was left.

Longthorpe Tower was a later addition to a fortified manor house. It is remarkable now for one of the finest examples of medieval domestic wall paintings in northern Europe, which were discovered under numerous coats of whitewash in 1946.

In Huntingdon and Cambridge the original mottes of their former castles are still clear to see, but in neither case do any of the buildings survive. **Cambridge Castle** was built by the Normans in 1068. In typical Norman style, twenty-seven houses were demolished to make way for it. The original structure was a motte and bailey type, made of wood. It was later rebuilt in stone during the reign of Edward I. The castle gradually decayed and its stone was plundered for building the university colleges. By 1590, it was described as 'old decayed and ruined'. The castle was briefly brought back to life during the Civil War, but soon the only part left was the gatehouse, which was used as a prison. This was demolished in 1842 to make way for a courthouse, which was itself demolished in 1954. All traces of the castle buildings have now disappeared and only the motte, called Castle Mound, survives. Shire Hall, built in 1930, stands on the northern half of the bailey site.

WEST VIEW OF THE GATE OF CAMBRIDGE CASTLE, CAMBRIDGESHIRE.

The site of **Huntingdon Castle** was probably first fortified by the Vikings, who occupied the town until they were driven out by Edward the Elder in AD 921. It was William the Conqueror who ordered the building of the first proper castle in 1068, soon after becoming King. It was a motte and bailey type castle, built of wood with a large defensive ditch on three sides and the River Ouse on the other. Twenty houses were demolished to make way for the new castle.

A hundred years later, the castle belonged to William I of Scotland, who was also Earl of Huntingdon. He sided with rebels against Henry II. The King himself besieged the castle for a month and once it fell he ordered it to be destroyed. It was pulled down with large iron hooks and probably burnt; archaeologists found a large amount of ash on the site.

The site was refortified as a gun platform during the English Civil War, but it was never rebuilt. A windmill was built on the top of the motte at some point, depicted in some eighteenth- and nineteenth-century sketches and paintings of the place, but no trace remains today apart from a clearly visible cart track which once led up to it. A large part of the outer bailey area was destroyed when the railway was built across the corner of the site in 1847.

Wisbech's 'Castle', which stands opposite Museum Square, is the latest of many different incarnations. There may have been some sort of fortification here in Saxon times to protect the area from the Danes, but it was William I who ordered the construction of a stone castle to defend communications between the Fens and the sea. The Fens were one of the last strongholds of the Saxons led by Hereward the Wake.

Wisbech Castle was a building of some importance in medieval times. It was whilst on his way to Wisbech that King John lost his wagons full of treasure and other possessions near the Wash. Edward I also stayed at Wisbech several times. The whole town and the castle were destroyed by sea flooding in 1236, but the castle at least was soon restored. It also served as a prison; in 1314 the Bishop of Glasgow and the wife of Robert the Bruce were held there.

By the late fifteenth century rebuilding was needed and Bishop, later Cardinal, Morton, Henry VII's Lord Chancellor, undertook the task as well as overseeing drainage work in the Fens. Most Bishops of Ely used the building as a palace while visiting Wisbech.

As in earlier times, the building was used as a prison, with over thirty Roman Catholic recusants held here during the reign of Elizabeth I.

The third building to occupy the site was a mansion built in 1656 for John Thurloe, Oliver Cromwell's Secretary of State. The medieval castle had not been attacked during the Civil War but it was dismantled or destroyed by the Parliamentarians. Thurloe's mansion was a building similar to Thorpe Hall in Peterborough, these being two of a very few mansions built during this period. Thurloe had very little opportunity to enjoy his new house though because on the Restoration of Charles II in 1660, ownership reverted to the Bishops of Ely.

In 1793 the Bishop sold the whole site to a London developer named Joseph Medworth for £2,305. He put more than fifty houses on the site, building the Crescent, York Place, Ely Place and Union Place. The mansion was offered to the Corporation of Wisbech for the Grammar School, but they disapproved of his plans, so it was demolished and replaced with a smaller Regency villa. This later house was, at one time, the residence of F.W. Bradley, a manufacturer and supplier of artificial teeth. Most recently it has been used as an education centre.

HOUSES AND HOMES

One of the buildings of most interest in Huntingdonshire is **Hemingford Grey Manor House**, which dates from the mid-twelfth century and is the oldest continuously inhabited secular building in England. It has been associated with many famous names. John Dudley, who would later become Duke of Northumberland, sold it to Richard Cromwell. Many years later it became the home of the novelist Lucy Boston, who used it as the inspiration for her Green Knowe children's stories.

Almost as old is the so-called **School of Pythagoras** in Cambridge. Despite its name, it was in all probability a large private house built from clunch rubble by the end of the twelfth century. A contract survives from 1373 for the rebuilding of its western end. A teacher called Newton Bosworth rented the building in 1808 and briefly turned it into an actual school for boy boarders. St John's College bought the building from Oxford's Merton College in 1959 and used it for a range of public readings, lectures and theatrical performances. In 2014 it was converted to an archives' repository and today it houses the irreplaceable archives of St John's College.

There are surprisingly few large and impressive stately homes in Cambridgeshire. **Wimpole Hall** is the largest such home in the old county of Cambridgeshire and is now owned by the National Trust. Wimpole was originally built in about 1640 for Sir Thomas Chicheley but it was extensively altered from the beginning of the eighteenth century onwards. The chapel and library were designed by renowned architect James Gibbs, who is famous for St Martin-in-the-Fields in London and the Radcliffe Camera in Oxford. From 1767 until 1773, Sir Lancelot 'Capability' Brown carried out a thorough landscaping of the house's grounds and gardens, although its main feature, the 2-mile-long south avenue across the estate, had existed since at least the 1720s. A mock ruined medieval castle, including a four-storey Gothic tower, was built at Wimpole in the 1770s.

Madingley Hall was possibly built just as an extravagant hunting lodge by one John Hynde in 1543. It soon became the family's main residence, however. A later owner remodelled it and removed the medieval village street so the houses wouldn't

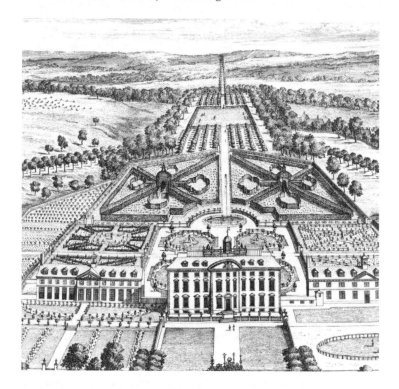

spoil his view. In 1861 it was rented by Queen Victoria for her son Edward whilst he was studying at Cambridge. His stay was cut short though by the death of his father, Prince Albert. The Hall was sold to the University of Cambridge in 1948 and is now the home of its Institute of Continuing Education.

Peckover House in Wisbech was built shortly before 1727 and from the late eighteenth century was the home of the wealthy Quaker banking family of Peckover. Whilst they lived there it was known as Bank House and it formed part of a row of impressive Georgian properties on the North Brink in Wisbech. The Peckovers' bank ultimately became part of Barclays Bank in 1896, while the house itself was donated to the National Trust in 1943 by Alexandrina Peckover, the last descendant of Jonathan Peckover, founder of the bank. In 1970 the supernatural story writer John Gordon used Peckover House as the inspiration for his eerie novel *The House on the Brink*.

Elton Hall and **Abbots Ripton Hall** are the only large houses still in private ownership in Huntingdonshire, as Hinchingbrooke House, Ramsey Abbey and Kimbolton Castle have all become schools. Paxton Park and Conington Castle have been demolished and other large houses turned over to corporate use.

The most impressive of these is Elton Hall, which has belonged to the Proby family since the 1660s. Members of the Proby family were adept at marrying heiresses, which gave them the funds to make changes to the Hall over the years, including the Gothic elements added in the eighteenth century. The Hall is home to many fine paintings, French furniture and one of the best libraries in private hands, which includes a copy of Henry VIII's prayer book, given to him by his sixth wife, Catherine Parr. The Hall lies in 200 acres of parkland.

Abbots Ripton Manor was mentioned in the Domesday Book. It was attached to the Abbey at Ramsey and passed into private hands after the Dissolution. It was sold in the mid-eighteenth century by the Lord of the Manor, one Julius Caesar! The Hall and manor became the property and second residence of the Fellowes family, Lords de Ramsey, whose main home was at

Ramsey Abbey. Abbots Ripton Hall was used as a Red Cross Hospital during the First World War and in 1936 the de Ramseys moved there permanently.

These days, Abbots Ripton is best known for its gardens and as the venue for the Secret Garden Party music festival hosted in the grounds between 2004 and 2017.

Hinchingbrooke and Ramsey Abbey were once owned by the Cromwell family but soon passed out of the family. Building at **Hinchingbrooke House** was begun by Oliver Cromwell's great-grandfather Richard, whose initials still remain on the great stone fireplace at first floor level in the north wall of the chapel. Most of the building work at Hinchingbrooke, however, was carried out by Sir Henry and Sir Oliver Cromwell. Sir Henry transported the late medieval gateway from Ramsey Abbey and re-erected it to the north-east of the house, while the great bow window on the eastern side of the house was added by Sir Oliver in 1602. Queen Elizabeth I came to Hinchingbrooke, King James I was a regular visitor, and Oliver Cromwell played there as a child. Hinchingbrooke House left the Cromwell family in 1627 when Sir Oliver sold it to Sir Sidney Montagu, a relative of the Kimbolton Montagus. Sir Sidney's descendants, the Earls of Sandwich, lived there for many generations but sold it to Huntingdonshire County Council in the 1960s. The house is now the sixth form block of Hinchingbrooke School.

Some buildings are of interest more for their inhabitants than their architecture. The Rectory in St Mary's Street, Ely, is celebrated as the home of Oliver Cromwell for ten or eleven years after 1636. After Cromwell's time it was briefly an inn, The Cromwell Arms, before reverting to its original purpose as a vicarage. The house was 'restored' at the beginning of the twentieth century according to the Victorian fashion of imitating the Tudor half-timbered style. **Cromwell's House** is now the Tourist Information Centre for the city of Ely as well as being a tourist attraction in its own right.

Sycamore Farm in Brampton near Huntingdon is better known as **Pepys' House**. The house belonged to Pepys' uncle and the diarist probably stayed there as a child when he attended the local grammar school. It passed to his father and then Pepys himself, but it never seems to have become his permanent home.

Although parts of the house date from the sixteenth century, it is really the association with the famous diarist that make it remarkable.

Inside the grounds of Impington Hall is **Impington Village College,** designed in 1938 by famous architects Walter Gropius and Maxwell Fry. Village colleges were the brainchild of Henry Morris, Chief Education Officer for the county, and were unique to Cambridgeshire. They were intended to be a central facility serving a number of local communities and would provide all their educational and cultural needs in one building, including libraries, clinics and education, from cradle to grave. Today they have become secondary schools, but they still provide educational and leisure facilities to adults out of school hours. The first to open was Sawston Village College in 1930; the most recent, Cambourne Village College, opened in September 2013.

Sawston Hall is distinguished by the role it played in the accession of Queen Mary I. Mary Tudor took refuge at Sawston Hall when her brother King Edward VI died. She evaded capture, disguised as a dairymaid according to tradition, rallied support across the country and claimed her throne from Lady Jane Grey, who had been proclaimed queen by the Protestants. Sawston Hall was set ablaze by those in pursuit. Mary rewarded the owners of the Hall, the Huddleston family, with a knighthood and honours at court. She also authorised the rebuilding of the Hall with clunch stone from Cambridge Castle, which is why Sawston Hall is the only Elizabethan mansion in Cambridgeshire to be built of stone and not brick.

Mary re-imposed Catholicism and expelled all but three of the Masters of the Cambridge University Colleges. Three Cambridge alumni, Archbishop Thomas Cranmer and Bishops Hugh Latimer and Nicholas Ridley, were burned for heresy in Oxford. John Hullier, a Fellow of King's College and former curate of Babraham Church, was burned on Jesus Green in Cambridge on Maundy Thursday, 2 April 1556, the only Protestant martyr to be executed in Cambridge.

The Huddleston family of Sawston remained staunchly Catholic and suffered many fines through the years. This means that Sawston Hall remains a fine example of a Tudor manor house because they had no money to improve it. It also explains the presence of the priests' hiding holes. One, hollowed out of the wall at the top of the tower, is 7ft long, 7ft high and 5ft wide; the entrance is concealed under the floorboards. It is said to be one of the finest examples of a priest hole in the country. There are three other hiding places in other parts of the house.

The Hall stayed in the Huddleston family until they sold it in 1982. During the Second World War it was used by the 66th Fighter Wing of the US 8th Air Force. It became the Cambridge Centre for languages and then passed into private hands and was restored.

THE UNIVERSITY OF CAMBRIDGE

Much of the outstanding architecture in and around Cambridge is, of course, due to the University, founded in 1209 when a group of students migrated there from Oxford after a dispute with the townspeople. The oldest surviving college is Peterhouse, founded in 1280. By the time of the Reformation, there were fifteen colleges at Cambridge and a further five were founded (or refounded) by 1600. The nineteenth and twentieth centuries then saw a huge and rapid increase in the size of the University. Today it has thirty-one colleges and over 100 academic departments.

King's College Chapel, the Wren Library at Trinity College and the Pepys Library at Magdalene College have already been mentioned in Chapter 2, but the University has many more architectural treasures.

The **Mathematical Bridge** at Queens' College was first designed in 1748 by the master carpenter William Etheridge and was built the following year by architect James Essex the Younger. According to legend, the bridge contained no fastenings but was instead just held together by pegging. Research shows, however, that this has never been the case. An old model of the bridge, probably built by William Etheridge himself to demonstrate the design, contains eyes for screws at the joints. The timber in Etheridge's bridge began to decay, so it was taken down and entirely rebuilt in 1867, together with the necessary fastenings. By the end of the nineteenth century the bridge's design was popularly attributed to Isaac Newton, but this was just another urban myth, too. Newton died in 1727, over twenty years before the bridge was built.

The main building of the **Fitzwilliam Museum** on Trumpington Street in Cambridge was completed in the 1870s, nearly sixty years after the founder's bequest. Its main staircase was created in a highly ornate and baroque style, popular with Victorian tastes at the time. By the time the museum was extended in the 1960s, tastes had changed and the extension was a simple white cube, with few windows. Today the museum receives about half a million visitors every year. Its support group, the Friends of the Fitzwilliam, was founded in 1909 and is the oldest known museum friends' group in Britain.

Addenbrookes Hospital is one of the oldest hospitals in the country. Dr John Addenbrooke, a fellow of St Catharine's College, died in 1719 and left some money in his will to establish a teaching hospital in the town. Originally it was just a small building on Trumpington Street. This was largely knocked down and replaced by a new building on the same site in the 1820s and '30s. By the late twentieth century, this hospital was clearly not big enough and so an entirely new hospital was built from scratch on Hills Road, which opened in 1976. Over the years, further buildings have been added around the hospital and the entire area is now called the Cambridge Biomedical Campus. Addenbrookes is a world-class transplant centre and has many achievements to its credit, including the first ever liver transplant in Europe in 1968, the world's first combined heart, lung and liver transplant in 1986, the first combined liver and pancreas transplant in 1988 and the first multi-visceral transplant in the UK in 1994.

The University has always been interested in astronomy. During the late eighteenth century there was even an attempt to build an observatory on top of Great Gate, the main gatehouse at the entrance to Trinity College. In 1822–23, the University built the **Observatory** on Madingley Road. The main telescope was placed inside the central classical dome, while two other telescopes were located at the ends of the wings in order to determine the exact positions of stars and planets. Their alignment with true east and west needed to be accurate, so the main front of the observatory faces exactly south. The building now houses the Institute of Astronomy's library but there are still small telescopes elsewhere on the site.

In 1957 the **Mullard Radio Astronomy Observatory** was constructed on Barton Road. By carefully placing smaller aerials in the correct relationship with each other it is possible to 'see' radio wave data, just as if you were using a single large radio telescope. Cambridge was the first observatory to try this idea, which is now followed throughout the world. The technique is called radio aperture synthesis and was used to discover the first pulsars. In 1974 Anthony Hewish and Martin Ryle, based at the Mullard Observatory, were awarded the Nobel Prize for their work in developing radio aperture synthesis.

PUBS, INNS AND HOTELS

Many pubs claim to be the oldest in Cambridge, including the Green Dragon in Chesterton and the Pickerel in Magdalene Street.

The **Pickerel Inn** dates from the 1500s. Through the years it has been used as a brothel and an opium den. A Pickerel is a type of fish (pike).

The Eagle is another of the oldest pubs in Cambridge and is famous for being a gathering place for scientists from the Cavendish Laboratory. It was here in 1953 that Crick and Watson announced that they had cracked the secret of DNA. Before that, however, it was the meeting place for RAF and USAAF crews during the Second World War. In the RAF Bar you can still see memorabilia from the time and, more poignantly, the names and numbers of the men and squadrons who visited the pub to relax. The ceiling is covered with graffiti; names etched on the ceiling with cigarette lighters, candles and lipstick. The writing had all but disappeared, covered with nicotine stains from the countless cigarettes smoked in the bar, but it was noticed, restored and preserved as a memorial to those brave men.

The **White Horse Inn** on Castle Street in Cambridge was built during the seventeenth century and was a coaching inn serving the turnpike road to Huntingdon and the North.

It closed in 1934 and the following year was rented by the newly established Cambridge and County Folk Museum Association with the aim of creating a museum devoted to Cambridgeshire life. The Association's members worked quickly and the new Folk Museum opened its doors to the public for the first time in November 1936. Folklorist Enid Porter served as curator for nearly thirty years, between 1947 and 1976, and over that time built up an unrivalled collection of objects evocatively illustrating the everyday life, customs and traditions of local people over the previous three centuries. The museum today is called the **Museum of Cambridge** and in 2006 was shortlisted for the Gulbenkian Prize for museum of the year.

The **Black Bear Inn** in Market Street was used by the Grand Committee of the Eastern Association during the English Civil War. Oliver Cromwell would have been one of the officers attending those meetings. The inn was demolished in 1848, but recently a Blue Plaque was unveiled by Sir John Major and placed in Market Passage to commemorate Cromwell and his association with the former inn. Samuel Pepys was also a visitor to the Black Bear; he stayed there in 1662.

Another inn associated with Cromwell is **The Falcon** in Huntingdon. It stands in the Market Square and parts of it date from the late sixteenth century. It is said that Cromwell addressed his troops in the square below from the bow window on the first floor.

For a Puritan, Cromwell is linked with a surprising number of drinking places. It is said that he, or a mistress he is supposed to have had, haunts the **Golden Lion Hotel** in St Ives, particularly around Room 13.

10

ROAD AND RAIL

ANCIENT ROADS

Having no mountains to speak of, the main barriers to communications across prehistoric Cambridgeshire were rivers, and so the routes of the main prehistoric trackways were determined by where the rivers could be crossed easily. Settlements grew up at these places and along the edge of the fens. The most ancient track was the **Icknield Way,** which passed through the southern part of the county on its way from the Thames Valley towards East Anglia, making use of the natural chalk ridge. Parallel to the Icknield Way was **Ashwell Street,** which followed the line of natural springs along the base of the chalkstone. Bronze axes have been found along both these routes, demonstrating their great age, and similar axes have been found elsewhere in the county, indicating a dense network of smaller tracks criss-crossing ancient Cambridgeshire and Huntingdonshire.

THE ROMANS

Both the Icknield Way and Ashwell Street were taken over by the Romans and incorporated into the vast system of metalled all-weather roads that was established after the invasion and which still lies under many of the roads we use today. Most of the other major Roman roads were new and laid out as sequences of short straight sections. **Ermine Street** stretched northwards from Royston towards Godmanchester (the route of today's A1198) and on to the fort of Durobrivae at Water Newon on the River Nene (part of the Great North Road, today's A1). The **Via Devana** connected Cambridge to Godmanchester (part of the A14). **Akeman Street** began at Wimpole and went to Cambridge (the A603), then via Ely and Littleport to Denver in Norfolk (the A10). **Worsted Street** ran from Wandlebury towards Horseheath and Haverhill (the A1307). There were many others.

The Romans also built extensive canals across the county, to provide bulk transport for the salted meat they supplied their troops with and which came from the imperial estates in the Fens. Canals were built between the 'islands' of March, Stonea and Whittlesey and another canal, part of today's **Car Dyke**, ran from Cottenham to Waterbeach and may have extended further.

After the end of Roman occupation, the canals silted up and the roads fell into disrepair. The outbreak of fighting between the former Romano–British population and the invading Anglo–Saxon tribes did not help either, as at times it was clearly more important to block the possible movement of people than to encourage it. The old Icknield Way, in particular, formed a natural invasion route for armies marching east or west, so it was comprehensively blocked by a system of dykes, the most famous of which is the 7-mile-long **Devil's Dyke**. Five such dykes survive and they are impressive structures formed of deep ditches and high earth banks. Archaeological investigation has shown that Fleam Dyke was the first to be built, immediately after the Roman evacuation. It was reconstructed twice during the Anglo–Saxon wars of the fifth and sixth centuries and only fell out of use during the seventh century.

TURNPIKE ROADS

During the Middle Ages, roads became the responsibility of local parishes. Every parish appointed one of its residents to be the '**surveyor of the highways**' for a year. It was a thankless and widely resented duty but it had to be done. The surveyor's main job was to organise the men of the parish to spend two full days each year in road maintenance and repair, such as moving fallen trees, clearing drainage ditches and laying down fresh gravel. As you can imagine, this often resulted in road repairs of the most amateurish quality. Parishes that combined very long roads with tiny populations, such as many Fenland parishes, ended up with roads hardly worth the name. Occasionally, if a road was blocked by a particularly large fallen tree then the dead tree would be left there and people would veer around it, creating a new path. Over time, this new path would itself become 'the road'. Even after the tree itself had decayed away, the road would keep its rather pointless-looking bend permanently.

This all started to change during the seventeenth and eighteenth centuries. Traders who were beginning to understand market economics wanted to connect their products with customers across the country but the existing road infrastructure was simply not up to the job. So **turnpike roads** were invented. These roads were highways that had been removed from local parish control and handed over to independent trusts, who were allowed to charge a fee for using the road. This fee would pay the wages and costs of the trustees and their staff, and any money left over would go towards keeping the road in good repair. The very first turnpike road in Britain, set up in 1663, was the Great North Road between Wadesmill in Hertfordshire and Stilton in Huntingdonshire. Soon many other roads across Cambridgeshire and Huntingdonshire were turnpiked.

THE COMING OF THE RAILWAY

Cambridgeshire benefited not only from being flat (and therefore a cheap place to build railways) but also from its situation between London and the North. In 1845, the Eastern Counties Railway opened its station at Cambridge, which lay on the new line from Liverpool Street Station to King's Lynn. Five years later its bitter rival, the Great Northern Railway, opened its own line from King's Cross to Peterborough and York, with stations at Huntingdon and St Neots. Working hard to increase their market share, the Eastern Counties Railway created a complicated network of local railway companies across Cambridgeshire and the Fens, which all fed traffic to the Cambridge line.

However, the unique geography of Cambridgeshire's Fenland, the fact that its towns and villages are on top of hills while the surrounding countryside is much lower, has caused occasional infrastructure problems. The nineteenth-century railway companies, in particular, found it very difficult to link the settlements together. Ideally a village railway station should be as close to the village centre as possible, but in the Cambridgeshire Fens that would have meant creating many unacceptable gradients because the railway line would need to rise up and down each hill. It was far cheaper to build the lines only along the flat countryside, but this meant that often the stations were built a long walk from the settlements they were supposed to serve. Stretham railway station, for example, was nearly 2 miles from the village of Stretham itself. Fenland village stations were therefore usually isolated and exposed to chill winds and rain blowing from the north and east. Passengers eventually preferred bus services, which travelled from door to door, and it was no surprise that many railway lines across the Fens were closed during the 1960s.

Cambridge railway station was built a long way from the city centre, a fact not really due to any active anti-railway efforts by the University but more because of the high cost of land in the centre of such a congested city. Occasional later efforts

by railway companies to build a much more compact central station, such as the proposal to build a small line crossing Jesus Green were, however, definitely frustrated by the University. The University was concerned about its students bunking off to London by train and the original Act setting up the station even had a clause allowing University authorities to inspect platforms for scholars.

Despite its distance from the centre, Cambridge station proved very popular and within two years of its opening, plans had already been drawn up to enlarge its platforms. By 1900, Cambridge station had become the city's second largest employer after the University itself. The station currently has the third longest platform in Britain, at 470m; only Gloucester and Colchester have longer platforms.

Cambridgeshire in the early twentieth century had a plethora of small stations. Despite St Ives being a market town and therefore dependent on transportation, the platform at **St Ives station** on the line to Huntingdon was so small that trains could not be any longer than three carriages. The line crossed many small wooden bridges on its way to Huntingdon; bridges which, alarmingly, often caught fire during dry summers.

TRAMS

Wisbech was notable for having a dedicated tramway. It was opened in 1883 by the Great Eastern Railway in order to carry agricultural produce between Wisbech and Upwell in Norfolk and had many sidings along its length so that food could be loaded onto the trains. The rails were set at the same gauge as proper railway lines, so in theory it could have been operated by a normal steam locomotive, but the continual stop-start operations over short distances meant that it was more economical to use trams instead. At that time, the crossing over the Wisbech canal was a humpbacked bridge, which gave the tramway engines a lot of work to do. The passenger service closed in 1927 and the line itself was shut in 1966, by which time most agricultural produce was being moved by lorry.

Cambridge briefly had a tram network, too, which linked the railway station with East Road and Market Hill. The tramway was first opened to traffic, with a horse-drawn tramcar, in October 1880. It kept going into the twentieth century but in 1908 double-decker buses were introduced by a competing bus company and the trams started to lose money. The final tram journey was made on 18 February 1914, after which the tramway's assets, including all the horses, were sold off.

Another tramway operated in **Peterborough**. The tram system began in 1903 and kept going right through until 1930. The trams started on Long Causeway near the Cathedral, then turned either north-east towards Newark or north-west up Lincoln Road to Dogsthorpe. A planned extension south of the Cathedral, to bring in Woodston and Fletton, was never built.

THE NENE VALLEY RAILWAY

Another line that shut following the Beeching 'axe' was between Peterborough and Yarwell Junction. This closed in 1972, but it was lucky enough to be given a new lease of life as the **Nene Valley Railway**. In 1974 the Peterborough Development Corporation leased the line to the Peterborough Locomotive Society so that they could run their restored BR Standard Class 5 locomotive along it. Over time, the Nene Valley Railway grew into one of the country's most popular historic lines; it has acquired many more steam locomotives from across Europe and the line itself has been extended so that it is over 7 miles long.

Cambridgeshire's newest railway station is **Cambridge North**. This opened in 2017 and is on the site of the old Chesterton village station, which operated very briefly in 1850. The modern station is handy for travellers visiting Cambridge's science and business parks.

THE BUSWAY

Cambridgeshire's main claim to transport fame today is the **Guided Busway**. This runs for 16 miles between Cambridge and St Ives and is the longest busway in the world – the second longest is in Australia and is only 7 miles. Construction began in 2007 and was completed four years later, by which time costs had tripled to an eye-watering £181 million. The busway runs for most of its length along the line of the old Cambridge to St Ives railway. The railway route was not wide enough simply to tarmac and turn into a road, which is why the buses have to be guided, so that they do not run the risk of driving into another bus coming the other way.

The busway has proved to be immensely popular with the public but it frequently appears in the news. The main problem is drivers of cars and vans who fail to spot the No Entry signs and try to drive onto the busway. There are car traps at most junctions and so their vehicles get stuck. Buses are sometimes held up if horses have wandered onto the line and there have been occasional incidents where bus drivers themselves have driven too quickly for the track, causing their buses to derail.

WATER TRAFFIC

The roads may have been poor during the Middle Ages but Cambridgeshire was certainly lucky with its rivers. The county had many inland ports and even Cambridge itself was a major port, relying heavily on barges to provide all the goods for Stourbridge Fair. Villages that were not situated directly on rivers built canals to link them to this traffic. All this industry vanished when the railways came, but some relics of the old ports remain, such as part of a seventeenth-century wharf at Mepal and the overgrown dock at the north end of Swavesey.

The city of Cambridge, of course, is known for **punting**. A punt is a flat-bottomed boat with a square-cut bow and which is propelled by a pole. Punts can only be used in shallow water (otherwise the pole will not work). They are different from Venetian-style gondolas, which are propelled by an oar.

Originally punts were used for angling and fowling but from the 1860s they were used on the Thames for leisure and by the 1880s there were leisure punts in Oxford. Punts did not arrive in Cambridge until the early twentieth century but they then became very popular and today it is believed that there are more punts on the River Cam than on any other river in Britain. An attempt was made in 1961 to introduce fibreglass punts but they did not stand up to the wear and tear.

Famously, Cambridge punts and Oxford punts are propelled from different ends of the boat. The Oxford punter stands inside the boat whereas in Cambridge the punter stands on the flat deck. Strictly speaking Cambridge is the 'wrong' end, because the early working punts used by fowlers and anglers were all propelled by the punter standing inside the boat and the decks were not strong enough to stand on. One elderly boat man, Don Strange, interviewed in the 1970s, claimed the change came about because female students at Girton College wanted to show off their ankles.

11

BURIED TREASURE

In the past, people believed that hoards of coins and other valuables had been buried in the ground for safekeeping, with the owner planning to return for them at a later date. This is certainly the case with the coins buried in **Brampton**. Samuel Pepys' diary entry for 13 June 1667 records a request to his wife to carry a stash of gold coins to Brampton and bury them in the garden. There was a strong fear of the Dutch invading London after seizing the warship HMS *Royal Charles* at Chatham. Pepys returned to Brampton in October to search for the coins at dead of night. He recovered them, but found that twenty-five were missing. As his wife and father had buried them in broad daylight, perhaps this is not surprising.

More recently, archaeologists have suggested that many coin hoards may have been left as offerings to the gods.

A hoard of sixty-seven Iron Age gold coins were discovered with a metal detector close to the village of **Kimbolton** in 2010. One of the coins was a quarter stater from the reign of King Cunobelin, ruler of the Catuvellauni in the first century AD. The Catuvellauni tribe covered roughly the area of Hertfordshire, Cambridgeshire, Bedfordshire and Buckinghamshire, and had their capital at St Albans. Cunobelin also ruled the Trinovantes, who lived in Suffolk and Essex, with their capital at Colchester.

This find is significant because coins were not used regularly for everyday transactions at that time. Coins only became more widely used after the Roman invasion of AD 43 because the soldiers were paid with coins. Obviously, this period was a time of great upheaval and uncertainty, so someone may have wanted to hide the coins or have made an offering to the gods for the return of peace.

Coins from a similar period were discovered near **March** in 1982 by a farmer planting an apple tree. The Field Baulk Hoard consisted of 872 silver coins minted by the Iceni tribe, which had been placed in a round pot. It is believed that the coins were buried at the time of Boudicca's revolt.

A similar number of bronze coins, 865, this time dating from the late Roman period, were discovered at Tiled House Farm in **Stretham**. There are remains of a Roman villa nearby. The hoard is now preserved at the Museum of Archaeology and Ethnology in Cambridge.

Roman coins were also found at **Woodwalton** in 1886. The coins were discovered in two smashed pots about half a mile south of the village, near the railway. By the time the *Victoria County History*'s account of Roman Huntingdonshire was published in 1926 the coins could no longer be traced, but other isolated coins found in Woodwalton date from the third quarter of the third century.

In February 1975 a hoard of fourth-century silver was found near **Water Newton**, site of the Roman town of Durobrivae. The twenty-seven silver and one gold piece are thought to be the earliest examples of Christian church silver discovered anywhere in the Roman Empire. Because of their importance, the items are now held in the British Museum.

The largest hoard ever discovered in the county was found in **Cambridge** on the corner of Magdalene Street and Chesterton Lane. The coins were found during work on Cambridge's sewer system by Anglian Water in October 2000. At the bottom of the hole dug by the engineers was a prehistoric river channel. Above that was a Roman road and part of an Anglo–Saxon cemetery containing the decapitated skeletons of people who had been executed. The 1,805 silver and nine gold coins were found under the floor of a medieval building and were probably placed there in the 1350s, perhaps by a wealthy merchant, shortly after the Black Death. They had a face value of £10 3s 9d – around £5,000 in today's money. The hoard is now on display in the Rothschild Gallery at the Fitzwilliam Museum and was the inspiration for the novel *The Devil's Disciples* by Susanna Gregory.

During the building of Longstaff Way in **Hartford**, near Huntingdon, in 1964, workmen discovered two earthenware pots filled with 1,018 coins from the reigns of Henry VI, Edward IV, Richard III and Henry VII. The size of the hoard indicates a wealthy individual, and the relatively large number of foreign coins, eighty-four coins from Brabant in the Netherlands and two Portuguese coins, shows that he may have been a merchant trading abroad. The coins had been placed inside a cooking pot and the second pot had been placed over the top to seal it shut. Both were then wrapped inside a bag tied round with leather thongs and buried in the earth. Unfortunately, the mechanical digger that was excavating the ground in 1964 smashed both pots and scattered the coins, which had to be retrieved by sieving a ton of earth and finally going over everything with a military mine detector. The coins were declared Treasure Trove and are now held in the British Museum.

Much earlier, in 1874 and 1875, forty-one Tudor and Stuart gold coins were found by workmen demolishing buildings in the old court of **Pembroke College**, Cambridge. The coins had a face value of £35 7s 9d, and all derived from the Tower of London mint. They were probably concealed in the 1640s during the English Civil War, possibly so that they wouldn't be taken either by the King or by Parliament. Alternatively, they may have been buried for safekeeping by someone who knew that he would be away from the college for some time. The Master and most of the Fellows were ejected by order of Parliament in March 1644, after which the College was essentially unoccupied for nearly

a year, so a treasurer or bursar at the time may have decided to bury the coins secretly under the hall for their security. The College loaned the coins to the Fitzwilliam Museum in 1958.

Over 1,000 early fourteenth-century coins were found at **Gorefield** in 1998. The coins were probably buried around 1312–14, during the reign of Edward II. They included halfpennies and farthings, which is unusual because hoarders did not usually bother burying coins of such small denominations.

Over the years, hoards of weapons, coins and artefacts have also been unearthed at many places across the Fens, including Barway in Soham, Wilburton Fen (1882), Isleham (1959) and Reach Fen (1867). The coins at **Barway** were found at various times from 1958 onwards, the most recent find being in 2011, but they appear to have all come from an original single hoard of at least 450 Roman coins. They seem to have been deliberately buried during the troubles of the late second century.

In January 1882 a labourer was digging a narrow drainage channel through the earth in **Wilburton Rush Fen** when he found some bronze objects at a depth of about 2ft below ground level. They turned out to be Late Bronze Age weapons and ornaments, including axes, swords and no fewer than 115 spears. The Cambridge Antiquarian Society purchased the hoard in 1920 and secured it for the Museum of Archaeology and Ethnology. The **Reach Fen** hoard, uncovered in 1867, contained a variety of broken artefacts from the Late Bronze Age (about 1000 BC), including axes, swords, buttons, rings and knives.

The **Isleham** hoard comprised over 6,500 items and is by far the largest Late Bronze Age hoard ever discovered in England. It was found in December 1959 by brothers William and Arthur Houghton while ploughing. The treasure includes swords, spearheads, arrows, axes, knives, daggers, armour, vessels, harness fittings and many fragments of sheet bronze, suggesting that it was a Late Bronze Age smith's scrap metal stock, although no evidence of actual smithing was found. The metal had been stored inside a pottery-lined pit about 3ft across, full almost to the surface with bronzework. Some of the items recovered from the pit are on display at West Stow Anglo–Saxon Village outside Bury St Edmunds, while other items are in the Museum of Archaeology and Anthropology in Cambridge.

12

FICTIONAL CAMBRIDGESHIRE

FILM

Several films have been made using Cambridgeshire as a backdrop, many of which have faded from memory, such as *Scarlet Thread* of 1951, in which two villains team up to steal some jewellery. The heist goes wrong and the villains hide from the police in the grounds of Trinity College. Another largely forgotten movie is *The Nightcomers* of 1971, which was filmed at Sawston Hall and which starred, almost unbelievably, Marlon Brando and Thora Hird.

But other films shot in the county are genuine classics. The 1981 Oscar-winner *Chariots of Fire* included many scenes set in Cambridge, including shots of King's Parade and King's College Chapel. The famous run around Trinity College's Great Court

Trinity *College in the University of* Cambridge.

was not filmed there, however, but at Eton. Trinity College did appear in *The Man Who Knew Infinity* (2015) with Dev Patel and Jeremy Irons, about Indian mathematician Srinivasa Ramanujan. St John's College has appeared in *The Theory of Everything* (2014) with Eddie Redmayne, *Elizabeth: The Golden Age* (2007) with Cate Blanchett, *The History Boys* (2006) with Richard Griffiths, and had a starring role in the video for Pink Floyd's 1994 single 'The Division Bell'.

Elizabeth: The Golden Age was also partly filmed at Ely Cathedral, where it was dressed to be the interior of Whitehall Palace. Ely Cathedral appears in many more films than you might think, including no fewer than two movies starring Michael Fassbender, namely *Macbeth* (2015) and *Assassin's Creed* (2016). One of the earliest stars to film at Ely was Al Pacino, who came to make the 1980 blockbuster *Revolution*, where the town appeared as eighteenth-century Philadelphia.

The Cathedral is often used as a setting for royal dramas, such as *The Other Boleyn Girl* (2008) with Natalie Portman, Scarlett Johansson and Eric Bana, and the Netflix TV series *The Crown* (2016 onwards) with Claire Foy and Matt Smith. In *The Crown*, the wedding of the young Princess Elizabeth to Prince Philip was re-enacted at Ely. In *The King's Speech* (2010) with

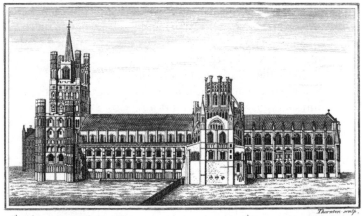

South Prospect *of the* CATHEDRAL CHURCH *of* ELY, *in* Cambridgeshire

Colin Firth, the Octagon crossing and front of the nave were transformed into the interior of Westminster Abbey at the time of the coronation of King George VI.

Ely Cathedral has even appeared in science fiction. The big budget flop *Jupiter Ascending* (2015) starring Mila Kunis and Eddie Redmayne included a spectacular wedding ceremony filmed in the nave, which was digitally enhanced to make it look futuristic.

Another Cambridgeshire location that has appeared in many films is the airfield at Duxford. The 1969 film *Battle of Britain* was largely made there, for obvious reasons, but Duxford also appeared during the 1960s in the Frank Sinatra spy caper *The Naked Runner* (1967) and the Michael Caine thriller *Billion Dollar Brain* (1966), in which it doubled for the icy Arctic in one scene. More recently, Duxford has appeared in the David Mitchell and Robert Webb comedy film *Magicians* (2007) and the Second World War movie *The Monuments Men* (2014) with George Clooney. The B–17 Flying Fortress movie *Memphis Belle* (1990) was also shot at Duxford, but the original movie on which it was based, *The Memphis Belle* of 1944, was filmed at Bassingbourn airfield while it was still an American bomber airbase. Bassingbourn also appeared in Stanley Kubrick's Vietnam War drama *Full Metal Jacket* (1987), where the barracks doubled as part of the US Marines' training camp.

Tom Cruise's excellent stunt at the beginning of *Mission Impossible: Rogue Nation* (2015), in which he hangs on to the outside of an Airbus A400 as it takes off, was filmed at RAF Wittering, near Peterborough.

The Nene Valley Railway (NVR) often appears on film and TV. It had a particularly notable appearance in the 1983 James Bond film *Octopussy*, in which it doubled as a railway crossing the border between East and West Germany. A decade later the NVR appeared in another James Bond film, *Goldeneye* (1995), in which an armoured Russian train was blown up on the track.

The rural French wartime scenes in *Atonement* (2007) with Keira Knightley and James McAvoy were shot at Coates and the Nene Washes.

Probably the most unlikely location was the use of the railway line at Bartlow for a jungle scene and steam train wreck in the

X-rated war comedy *The Virgin Soldiers* in 1968, with Hywel Bennett and Nigel Davenport. The Bartlow section of the line used to run between Cambridge and Saffron Walden, but the line closed in 1967 as part of the Beeching cuts. That meant that the film-makers could easily shoot there without disrupting any real-life train services. The line was dressed to make it look like the Malaysian jungle around Singapore (really!) and an old LMS locomotive, Black 5 no. 44781, was deliberately derailed and hung off the track at an angle. After filming was completed, an antique dealer from Saffron Waldon purchased the engine but he could not raise enough money to cover the British Railways charge for re-railing it. The engine was sold for scrap and cut up on site.

TV

Douglas Adams' *Dirk Gently's Holistic Detective Agency* was set in Cambridge at the fictional St Cedd's College. He also wrote an episode of *Doctor Who* ('Shada') set in his home city. The Doctor, Tom Baker, and company finished filming in Cambridge in 1979, but the episode was never finished due to a BBC studio strike. It was finally completed for download in October 2017.

Alan Partridge stays at the Linton Travel Tavern, which he claims is equidistant between Norwich and London, in the 1997 TV series *I'm Alan Partridge*.

Most recently, the ITV detective series *Grantchester* staring James Norton and Robson Green has featured many local scenes. The village of Grantchester itself is used for many external scenes and the real Church of St Andrew and St Mary appears in the series, too. For some episodes, King's Parade in the centre of Cambridge is convincingly dressed to appear as it would have done in the 1950s.

WRITERS AND CHARACTERS

Turning to literature, Cambridgeshire has long appeared in stories. The White Horse pub in Eaton Socon (at that time in Bedfordshire, technically) is mentioned in Charles Dickens' *Nicholas Nickleby*. Incidentally, the manuscript of *Great Expectations* is in the Wisbech and Fenland Museum, bequeathed to the museum by the Reverend Chauncy Hare Townshend, a lifelong friend of Charles Dickens.

The most famous literary mention of any local place is probably the tiny village of Little Gidding, north of Huntingdon. A visitors' book, dated 1936, records a visit made by the poet Thomas Stearns Eliot to the church there, which had been established by Nicholas Ferrar in 1626. The church and its small Anglican community made such an impression on Eliot that it inspired him to write 'Little Gidding', the fourth and final poem of his *Four Quartets* series. Within the poem, the narrator meets a ghost that is a combination of various poets and literary figures. The commemorative large stone floor in honour of T.S. Eliot at Poet's Corner in Westminster Abbey is inscribed with a line from the poem.

Henry Graham Greene, or Graham Greene as he is better known, spent the better part of his childhood with his uncle in the Cambridgeshire village of Harston. His time there was so memorable that he said 'it was at Harston I found quite suddenly I could read – the book was Dixon Brett, Detective. I didn't want anyone to know of my discovery, so I read only in secret, in a remote attic...'

Novelist Tom Sharpe studied at Pembroke College and taught history at the Cambridge College of Arts and Technology. His novel, *Porterhouse Blue*, is set in Cambridge. Skullion, portrayed on TV by David Jason, was thought by some to have been modelled on Albert Jaggard, head porter at Corpus Christi. Sharpe himself lived for a time in Great Shelford.

Cambridge serves as the backdrop in the twenty-three medieval crime novels featuring physician Matthew Bartholomew by Susanna Gregory. Ariana Franklin, the pen name of novelist Diana Norman, who died in 2011, had a twelfth-century female healer as her crime-solving heroine, Adelia Aguilar, who lived near Cambridge. Alison Bruce's detective Gary Mayhew is more contemporary, based at the Parkside Police Station. In James Runcie's novels, the crime-solving hero is a vicar with a liking for beer and jazz, Sidney Chambers.

Dorothy L. Sayers' father was first the vicar of Bluntisham in the Huntingdonshire Fens and later Christchurch, so from an early age she was familiar with the landscape and character of the Fens. Her classic detective story *The Nine Tailors*, published in 1934, is set in the Fens. It features the famous upper-class detective Lord Peter Wimsey and is often considered to be her best work. The church in the novel is almost certainly based on St Peter and St Paul's at Upwell.

Another crime writer to be influenced by the Fens is the late P.D. James. Although born in Oxford, she lived in Cambridge for many years and went to Cambridge High School for Girls. Several of her novels are set wholly or partly in the Fens. The quintessential Fenland novel is *Death of an Expert Witness*, set in an imaginary forensic science laboratory near Ely and in the surrounding fen. James said: 'the Fenland could be an alien place to those who don't live there. I was anxious for its bleakness to add to the mystery.' It certainly does. Another of her novels, *An Unsuitable Job for a Woman*, is set in Cambridge.

Perhaps the most famous novel to be set in the Fens is *Waterland* by Graham Swift, a story about a man looking back on his childhood as the son of a Fenland lock-keeper. *Waterland* was first published in 1983 and has been widely recognised as one of the classics of twentieth-century British literature – it was shortlisted for the Booker Prize and won the Guardian Fiction Prize. The film made of *Waterland* starred Jeremy Irons.

Moving away from fiction, many factual writers have written about Cambridgeshire, too. Celia Fiennes (1662–1741), a contemporary of Daniel Defoe and daughter of a colonel in Cromwell's army, began her travels around the age of 22, 'to regain my health by variety and change of aire and exercise', and was very much of the opinion that everyone could benefit from the same: 'if all persons, both Ladies, much more gentlemen, would spend some of their tyme in journeys to visit their native Land [it] would be a sovereign remedy to cure or preserve from these epidemick diseases of vapours, should I add Laziness?'

Travelling on horseback, often in the company of just two servants, Celia visited every county in England, as well as making brief forays into Scotland and Wales. She first travelled through Cambridgeshire in 1697, passing through Babraham and Cambridge, which she initially dismissed with the comment that 'the Buildings are old and indifferent, the Streets mostly narrow'.

After a trip to Hinchingbrooke House, she proceeded, via Stilton, to Whittlesey Mere. Once one of lowland England's largest freshwater lakes, Celia found it an imposing sight:

> a great water on the right hand about a mile off which looked like some Sea it being so high and of a great length ... there is no coming near it in a mile or two, the ground is all wett and marshy but there are severall little channels run into it which by boats people go up to this place; when you enter the mouth of the Mer it looks formidable and is often very dangerous by reason of sudden winds that rise like Hurricanes in the Mer.

Celia Fiennes returned to the county the following year as part of 'My Great Journey to Newcastle and Cornwall', visiting Ely, which she described as 'only a harbour to breed and nest vermin in', Chippenham Park and Sutton.

In 1724, the popular writer Daniel Defoe (1661–1731), famous for his novel *Robinson Crusoe*, which had been first published five years earlier, began a tour of England and Wales. In the course of his travels he visited Huntingdonshire and Cambridgeshire, and his comments on places in both counties give a unique insight into how people lived at the time. In Stilton, for instance, Defoe noted that the cheese 'is brought to table with mites, or maggots round it, so thick, that they bring a spoon with them for you to eat the mites with, as you do the cheese.' Defoe also commented that the road south from Sawtry towards Huntingdon was 'famous for being the most noted robbing-place in all this part of the country'.

Defoe was more impressed with Portholme meadow at Huntingdon, however. 'Here are the most beautiful meadows on the banks of the River Ouse, that are to be seen in any part of England,' he wrote, 'and to see them in the summer season, covered with such innumerable stocks of cattle and sheep, is one of the most agreeable sights of its kind in the world.'

During the 1860s, Karl Marx, one of the founders of the international Communist movement, was living in London, where he spent much time writing *Das Kapital*, a monumental work on political economy. In that book, Marx specifically mentioned the poor-quality living conditions in some villages in Cambridgeshire and Huntingdonshire as part of the evidence for his economic arguments. He reserved his most critical comments for the village of Hartford, just to the east of Huntingdon. Marx wrote that:

> ...these allotments are at a distance from the houses, which are without privies. The family must either go to the allotment to deposit their ordures, or, as happens in this place, saving your presence, use a closet with a trough set like a drawer in a chest of drawers, and drawn out weekly and conveyed to the allotment to be emptied where its contents were wanted. In Japan, the circle of life-conditions moves more decently than this.

In 1901, Henry Rider Haggard (1856–1925), the famous author of swashbuckling adventure novels such as *She* and *King's Solomon's Mines*, travelled through Cambridgeshire and Huntingdonshire. In the village of Bluntisham he saw new cottages, which had been built to house agricultural labourers. They showed a marked improvement over the earlier cottages on which Marx had commented:

> They were very excellent dwellings erected with much taste, containing three bed and two sitting rooms. The great point about them was that they were roofed with the best of thatching material, sedge, which is warm in winter and very cool in summer, as I proved by visiting the top rooms on that scorching day... Of course its drawback is the liability to fire, but as Mr Tebbutt pointed out, there was no record in his neighbourhood of any life being lost through such an incident.

Earlier in his journey, Haggard had seen the sedge being cut at Wicken Lode in Cambridgeshire. 'Then came two barges laden with towering loads of brown sedge, that makes the best thatching in the world,' he wrote. 'Alas! the plant is growing rare. It takes four years to mature, and then, if good, fetches one pound a load.'

Cambridgeshire has also appeared in children's literature. Philippa Pearce lived in Great Shelford and her classic novel for children, *Tom's Midnight Garden* (1958), is set in the Mill House there. Cambridge appears as 'Castleford'.

Another author who set her children's books in a house she knew was Lucy Boston. The *Green Knowe* stories are based on her own house, Hemingford Grey Manor House, the oldest continually inhabited private house in the country. *The Children of Green Knowe* was first published in 1954 and five other novels then followed, with the last, *The Stones of Green Knowe*, published in 1976.

Stories about twins Topsy and Tim, the children who have had every experience known to man, were first published in the 1960s by Stretham authors Gareth and Jean Adamson. The twins have become beloved by a new generation, thanks to their exploits on CBBC.

Another CBBC favourite, *Thomas the Tank Engine*, was created by the Reverend Wilbert Vere Awdry. He was rector of the parish of Elsworth with Knapwell from 1946 to 1953 and then vicar of Emneth near Wisbech from 1953 to 1965. Awdry was a steam train enthusiast and he originally created the 'Railway Stories' in 1943 to amuse his son Christopher during a bout of measles. His stories were so popular that he continued writing and they were duly published. Christopher, who took over the writing of the stories, lived for several years at Stilton.

Jill Paton Walsh's *Gaffer Sampson's Luck* was set in the Fens around St Ives and John Rowe-Townsend's *The Xanadu Manuscript* was set in Cambridge. The illustrator of books for very young children, Jan Ormerod, lived for many years in Cambridge.

Finally, it was once argued that Thomas Malory, author of *Morte d'Arthur*, was a Cambridgeshire man, after a will of a Thomas Malory was uncovered in the archives at Lambeth Palace, dating from 1469. Very little information is known about this Papworth St Agnes Malory, although we do know that he was alleged to have ambushed and kidnapped the local parson and refused to release him unless the parson paid £100. Sadly, the Papworth St Agnes Malory was not a knight and so it is far more likely that the real Sir Thomas Malory was another person with the same name!

13

CAMBRIDGESHIRE WHO'S WHO

Famous individuals who have studied at Cambridge University could make up a whole book on their own. These are some of the other notable individuals who have called Cambridgeshire home.

Jeffrey and Mary Archer are both famous in their own right. They live at the Old Vicarage in Grantchester, about which Rupert Brooke famously wrote a poem. **Mary Archer** is a distinguished scientist and was Chairman of the Cambridge University Hospitals NHS Trust for ten years. Since 2015 she has been Chair of Trustees of the National Science Museum Group.

Jeffrey Archer is famous for losing a large amount of money in 1974 with bad investments and then recouping his fortune with a string of successful novels, beginning with *Not a Penny More, Not a Penny Less* published in Britain in 1976. He was Deputy Chairman of the Conservative Party in the mid-1980s and became a peer, but was tainted by scandal and served time in prison. He kept diaries while in jail, which he later published.

Richard Attenborough (1923–2014) was born in Cambridge, his father being a fellow of Emmanuel College. During the Second World War he served as a film-maker in the RAF and went on to be a successful actor and film director, starring in *The Great Escape* and *Jurassic Park*, and winning an Oscar for his direction of the film *Gandhi*. He also became President of RADA and BAFTA.

His younger brother **David Attenborough** (b. 1926) studied Natural Science at Clare College and became the most famous wildlife presenter in the world. The Centre for Biodiversity

Conservation on the New Museums Site at Cambridge University is named in his honour.

England footballer **Darren Bent** (b. 1984) attended Hinchingbrooke School in Huntingdon and started his playing career with Godmanchester Rovers. He scored his first international goal in 2010, playing against Switzerland in a Euro 2012 qualifier.

Rupert Brooke (1887–1915) is best remembered for his war poetry written during the First World War and, of course, the famous poem about Grantchester, 'The Old Vicarage', written in 1912. He studied at King's College and threw himself into Cambridge life. Encouraged by his friends, he developed an enthusiasm for long walks, camping, nude bathing and vegetarianism. Brooke became a member of the Cambridge Apostles, was elected President of the Cambridge University Fabian Society, helped found the Marlowe Society drama club and acted in plays including the Cambridge Greek Play.

At Grantchester, the Orchard became the meeting place for his Bohemian circle of friends, including Ludwig Wittgenstein, Bertrand Russell, Virginia Woolf, E.M. Forster and John Maynard Keynes. Keynes visited Brooke at Grantchester and found him 'sitting in the midst of admiring females with nothing on but an embroidered sweater'; in a letter to a girlfriend, Brooke confirmed that 'I wander about barefoot and almost naked ... I live on honey, eggs and milk, prepared for me by an old lady like an apple.'

This life came to an end when he enlisted at the start of the First World War and died of blood poisoning whilst sailing to Gallipoli. Described as the handsomest man in England, he became a symbol of England's tragic losses in the Great War.

Lancelot 'Capability' Brown was born on 30 August 1716. He acquired the nickname Capability because of his frequent assurances to clients that their land had the capability to be improved. He designed over 170 parks in the new style of the English landscape garden. In 1767 he bought an estate at Fenstanton in Huntingdonshire from the Earl of Northampton and was appointed High Sheriff of Cambridgeshire and Huntingdonshire in 1770. Brown died in 1783 and was buried in the churchyard of St Peter and St Paul, the parish church of his small estate at Fenstanton Manor.

Joe Bugner (b.1950), heavyweight boxing champion, fled his homeland of Hungary as a 6-year-old after the Soviet invasion of 1956 and ended up living in Huntingdonshire. He caught the boxing bug at Smithy's Gym in St Ives and found he had a talent for it. He fought for the world heavyweight championship in 1975 but lost on points in a second bout with Muhammad Ali.

Geoff Capes (b.1949), international shot-putter and winner of the 'World's Strongest Man' competition, lived in Brampton near Huntingdon, where he was a local policeman for ten years. He is the most capped British male athlete of all time, receiving sixty-seven international caps.

Edith Cavell (1865–1915), the First World War nurse who was executed by the Germans after saving the lives of soldiers in Brussels, was educated in Peterborough. She and her Belgian and French colleagues helped around 200 Allied soldiers escape from occupied Belgium. The city's hospital was named after her.

Thomas Clarkson was an English abolitionist and a leading campaigner against the slave trade in the British Empire. He was born in Wisbech in 1760, the son of a clergyman who also taught at the local grammar school. In 1779, Clarkson went to Cambridge University, where he won a Latin essay competition on the subject of whether it was lawful to make slaves of others against their will. Clarkson campaigned tirelessly against the slave trade for twenty years until it was finally abolished in 1807. In 1833 Parliament passed the Slavery Abolition Act, which gave all slaves in the British Empire their freedom and compensated their owners. Thomas Clarkson died in 1846. In 1880 a large monument, designed by Gilbert Scott, was erected in his memory in Wisbech.

Christopher Cockerell (1910–99), inventor of the hovercraft, was born in Cherry Hinton near Cambridge. His father Sydney was Director of the Fitzwilliam Museum and his mother Florence was a designer and illustrator. His parents often had distinguished guests visit but the young Christopher was more interested in machines; when T.E. Lawrence came to stay, he was only interested in Lawrence's 1,000cc Brough Superior motorcycle. Christopher went to St Faith's Primary School and then Gresham's School in Norfolk. He returned to Cambridge to read engineering at Peterhouse. During the Second World War he worked on radio communication and navigation equipment for the RAF and Royal Navy. In the 1950s he began work on designing the hovercraft.

Lord Protector after the Civil War and execution of Charles I, **Oliver Cromwell** is the only commoner ever to be offered the British crown. Oliver was born in Huntingdon in 1599 and represented the town as MP in 1628. In the early 1630s he fell on hard times and moved to St Ives. Oliver's luck changed when he inherited a property in Ely from his uncle. He was elected as an MP again in 1640 at the start of the Long Parliament, this time representing Cambridge. Despite having no previous military experience, he joined the Parliamentary forces at the start of the Civil War and rose to become their most successful commander. In 1653 he became Lord Protector and, effectively, King until his death in 1658. After the Restoration in 1660 Cromwell's body was exhumed from Westminster Abbey; its head was cut off and stuck on a pike. A head believed to have belonged to Cromwell is buried in the chapel of Sidney Sussex College in Cambridge.

Sidney Sussex College, Cambridge.

Charles Darwin (1809–82) was one of Cambridge University's most famous students. He did not make his home in the city, but his son Sir George Darwin lived at Newnham Grange, which was donated by the family for the foundation of Darwin College. The young Charles studied at Christ's College. From Cambridge he embarked on a groundbreaking journey of discovery around the world on HMS *Beagle* and, fifty years after his birth, his seminal work *On the Origin of Species* was published.

Darwin wrote 'the only evil I found in Cambridge, was its being too pleasant'. Cambridge introduced Darwin to the right people and it was here that he developed a passion for the natural sciences. It also brought him the most important opportunity of his life, the invitation to join HMS *Beagle*. His entire life thereafter was altered. He even continued to rise early in the morning, something that was popularly believed at the time to distinguish Cambridge from Oxford men.

Warwick Davis (b. 1970) has had a successful career in film and TV, including his role as an Ewok in the Star Wars films and as Professor Filius Flitwick in the Harry Potter films. He lived in the Cambridgeshire village of Yaxley for several years and often appeared at local functions. However, he was forced to leave the village after fans discovered his address and began pestering him for photos and autographs at home.

Charlotte Edwards (b. 1979), England Women's Cricket Captain, was born in Pidley and attended Somersham Primary, the Ailwyn and Ramsey Abbey Schools, as well as spending a year at Cambridge Regional College. She first started playing cricket at Ramsey Cricket Club and made her international debut in 1996, the youngest player ever to represent England.

Olympic swimmer and TV presenter **Mark Foster** (b. 1970) lived in St Neots for twenty years. He competed primarily in short distance butterfly and freestyle competitions. He is a former world champion and won multiple medals in international competition during his long career. In May 2009 Foster became patron of the Anaphylaxis Campaign, the charity for people with severe allergies.

The percussionist **Evelyn Glennie** (b. 1965) lives in Upton. Despite being deaf since her early teens, she became the world's only full-time professional solo percussionist. She performed at the opening ceremony of the Olympic Games in London and also opened the new Huntingdon Library in 2009. She has an office on Hinchingbrooke Business Park.

Sculptor **Antony Gormley** (b. 1950) lived in a cottage in Pampisford whilst an undergraduate at Trinity College. Several of his works may be seen in the city, including a model of the *Angel of the North* in the Fitzwilliam Museum. The *Free Object* on the Backs at Trinity is made from cast iron, a blockwork human figure 2.5 times life-size that weighs over 10 tonnes. DAZE IV is on the Sedgewick site and one of his 'Learning to See' sculptures (a single standing figure, with feet together and arms at its sides, based on a cast of his own body) is in the main library of Jesus College, where Sir Antony is an honorary fellow. The most intriguing is perhaps 'Earthbound: Plant', a life-size metal sculpture of the human form, which is buried upside down in front of the MacDonald Institute for Archaeological Research on the Downing Site, with only the soles of its feet visible.

Robbie Grabarz (b. 1987), an Olympic and European medal-winning high jumper, attended Crosshall and Longsands Schools in St Neots.

Dave 'Boy' Green (b. 1953), British and European Boxing Champion, was born in Chatteris. He attended the Cromwell School and joined the Chatteris Amateur Boxing Club but moved to St Ives when he had no one to spar with. He turned professional in 1974. The word 'Boy' was part of local dialect meaning 'mate' and had been used by another Chatteris boxer, Eric Boon, in the early stages of his career. He also had the nickname the 'Fen Tiger' and his punches were named 'The Muck-Spreader' and 'Carrot Cruncher' for the style and ferocity with which they were delivered.

Dave Greenfield (b. 1949), keyboard player with The Stranglers who created the melody for their 1981 hit 'Golden Brown', used to run the Windmill pub in Somersham.

Elizabeth and Maria Gunning were born in the 1730s in Hemingford Grey. They created a storm with their beauty when they appeared in London at the court of King George II and both married well – in fact, Elizabeth married two members of the aristocracy in succession, the Duke of Hamilton and the Marquess of Lorne, and for a while she was engaged to the Duke of Bridgwater, too. Maria died tragically young at the age of 27, probably poisoned by the lead and arsenic in the make-up she used rather liberally.

Peter Hall (1930–2017), founder of the Royal Shakespeare Company, was head boy at the Perse School and read English at St Catharine's College from 1950 to 1953. His father was a stationmaster and the family lived for some time at Great Shelford Station.

Octavia Hill (1838–1912) was born on South Brink, Wisbech. Her father was declared bankrupt in 1840, which gave Octavia first-hand experience of living in straitened financial circumstances. In 1851 the Hill family moved into London, where the grim urban poverty horrified Octavia. She went on to become a leading housing reformer of the time. She believed in 'the life-enhancing virtues of pure earth, clean air and blue sky' and in 1894 she became one of the co-founders of the National Trust. The Octavia Hill Society was set up in 1992 to promote awareness of Octavia's ideas and ideals and their relevance in today's society. Under the society's auspices her birthplace at Wisbech has been turned into the Octavia Hill Birthplace Museum.

Legendary cricketer **John (Jack) Hobbs** (1882–1963) was born in poverty in Brewhouse Lane, Cambridge. His father was groundsman at King's College, but the young Jack generally played on the public pitch at Parker's Piece. He went on to play for Surrey and in 1908 he made his Test debut for England. The First World War interrupted his career – he joined the Royal Flying Corps as a mechanic – but he returned to cricket afterwards and retired from the sport in 1931, having made 61,700 runs in first-class matches. Many contemporaries regarded him as the best batsman in the world.

Thomas Hobson (1544–1631), a livery stable owner in Cambridge in the late 1500s and early 1600s, is the originator of the phrase Hobson's Choice. He noticed that some horses were hired more than others and were often tired, so he began allowing only the horse nearest the door to be hired. Hobson was famous in Cambridge not just for his horses, but also for his philanthropy. He donated money to the Town and University to bring fresh water into the city centre, through a conduit, to a big fountain in Market Square. His inn was situated on the corner of Jesus Lane and King Street and is today called the Cambridge Brewhouse.

John Howland from Fenstanton was one of the Pilgrim Fathers who travelled to America aboard the *Mayflower* in 1620. During the voyage he was almost swept overboard but was pulled back in and arrived safely. He was the last surviving passenger, dying in 1673 aged about 80. His descendants are said to include Winston Churchill and US presidents Franklin Roosevelt, Richard Nixon, Gerald Ford, George and George W. Bush.

Jake Humphrey (b. 1978), TV sports presenter, was born in Peterborough. His family moved to Norfolk when he was 9. He has co-presented BBC Sports Personality of the Year and presented BBC's coverage of Formula One from 2009 to 2012.

Eglantyne Jebb (1876–1928), social reformer and founder of the Save the Children organisation, moved to Cambridge in 1894. In 1906 she compiled her book *Cambridge: A Brief Study in Social Questions*. After the First World War, with her sister Dorothy, she founded the Save the Children Fund.

The singer **Olivia Newton John** was born in Cambridge in 1948. During the Second World War her father had been an MI5 officer on the Enigma project at Bletchley Park and the officer who took Rudolph Hess into custody. After the war he became the youngest headmaster of a Cambridge grammar school. The family emigrated to Australia when Olivia was 5. She later became famous as the star of the 1978 film *Grease*.

John Maynard Keynes (1883–1946) was an economist whose ideas have changed the economic policies of governments. Keynesian economics advocate the use of fiscal measures to mitigate the effects of economic recession. Born in Cambridge in 1883, his father was also an economist and a lecturer at the University of Cambridge. His mother, Florence Ada Keynes, was a social reformer and the first female borough councillor in Cambridge. Keynes went to school at the Perse kindergarten and St Faith's before attending Eton. He returned to Cambridge to read maths at King's College and became President of the Cambridge Union Society and Cambridge University Liberal Club. Later Keynes worked for the Treasury and he criticised the huge war reparations that were imposed on Germany following the First World War. After the Second World War he worked on the post-war settlement and played a part in the setting up of the World Bank and the International Monetary Fund.

Hannah Tapfield King (1808–86) was born in Bene't Street, Cambridge. In her forties she was converted to the Mormon faith by her seamstress and although her husband, a farmer from Sawston, didn't join the faith, she persuaded him to sell up and emigrate with their children to America in 1853. They joined the pioneers travelling to Salt Lake City in Utah, where she acquired a reputation as a writer and poet. She 'married' Brigham Young in 1872 when aged 65, she was his 55th (and last) wife but she continued to live with her first husband, Thomas King, who died in 1874. Her son, Thomas Owen Junior, became a Pony Express rider.

John Major (b. 1943) was elected as MP for Huntingdon in the 1979 General Election. He succeeded Margaret Thatcher as Prime Minister from 1990 to 1997 and was knighted in 2005.

Aston Merrygold (b. 1988), member of the boy band JLS, was born in Peterborough and attended the Jack Hunt School.

Eastenders actor **Sid Owen** (b. 1972) lives in Alconbury. He played Ricky Butcher in the soap from 1988 to 2012.

Priscilla Peckover was born into a wealthy banking family in Wisbech on 27 October 1833 and died there in 1931. As a Quaker, she was opposed to all forms of war. In 1879 she formed the Women's Local Peace Association (later named the Peace Union), which had affiliated groups in thirty-one countries, to work for peace by means of arbitration and disarmament. She devoted much of her life to the peace movement, even during the First World War when pacifism was much frowned upon. She was shortlisted for the Nobel Peace Prize four times but did not win. Priscilla was also instrumental in having the Bible translated into the international language Esperanto.

Samuel Pepys (1633–1703), the famous diarist, was related to the Montagus of Hinchingbrooke House in Huntingdon through his great aunt Paulina. He was a frequent visitor to Huntingdon and the surrounding area and spent some time at the Huntingdon Grammar School. Pepys' great grandfather had married well and acquired the Manor of Cottenham. He studied at Magdalene College and left the college his library of 3,000 books and manuscripts.

Joe Perry (b. 1974) the snooker player was born in Wisbech. He is nicknamed the 'Fen Potter' and 'the Gentleman'. He is now based at WT's Sports Bar in Cambridge.

Pink Floyd band members Syd Barrett, David Gilmour and Roger Waters all have a connection with Cambridge. **David Gilmour** was born in Grantchester in 1946. His father was a professor of genetics and senior lecturer in zoology. He attended the Perse School and studied modern languages at the Cambridge School of Technology. David moved to 109 Grantchester Meadows in 1956 when he was 10 and later performed a song called 'Grantchester Meadows' (written by Roger Waters) for Pink Floyd's 1969 *Ummagumma* album. David Gilmour is estimated to be worth £78 million, ranking 861st on the *Sunday Times* Rich List.

Roger Keith 'Syd' Barrett was born in Glisson Road, Cambridge, in 1946. His father was a doctor at Addenbrookes Hospital. Syd lived at 183 Hills Road from the age of 3. After the death of his father and when his siblings moved out, his mother rented out rooms to lodgers, including the future Japanese Prime Minister. One story is that he acquired his nickname from a local double bassist, Sid 'the Beat' Barrett. Syd was educated at Morley Memorial Primary School and the Cambridge School of Art.

Syd was unable to cope with fame and developed a drug addiction. He left the band in 1968 shortly after Roger Gilmour joined it. He returned to Cambridge in the 1970s and lived a reclusive existence. Syd liked to drink quietly at The Rock pub just off Cherry Hinton Road, his watering hole until the end of his life in 2006.

George Roger Waters was born in Surrey in 1943 but moved to Cambridge in 1944. He lived with his mother, a schoolteacher, at 42 Rock Road in the early 1960s. Like Syd, he studied at the County High School (later known as Hills Road College), which Roger used as his inspiration for *The Wall* – 'Apart from games I loathed every second of it,' he said. He joined Pink Floyd in 1968, effectively taking over from Syd Barrett.

Enid Porter (1909–84) lived in Cambridge. Between 1947 and 1976 she was Curator of the Cambridge and County Folk Museum (now the Museum of Cambridge) on the junction of Castle Street and Northampton Street. She collected a vast amount of irreplaceable material relating to the county's people, their folk beliefs and customs, and published a number of books.

Michael Ramsey (1904–88) was born in Chesterton Lane, Cambridge, and also lived in Buckingham Road. He studied at Magdalene College and was at one time vicar at St Bene't's in Cambridge. He served as the 100th Archbishop of Canterbury from 1961 to 1974.

Neil Robertson (b. 1982) was born and raised in Melbourne, Australia, but is now based in Cambridge. He practised at the Cambridge Snooker Centre, but is now based at WT's Sports Bar in Cambridge, where he practises with Joe Perry. He was crowned snooker world champion in 2010.

Henry Royce (1863–1933) was born in Alwalton near Peterborough and was later apprenticed at the Great Northern Railway Works in the city. He set up a successful engineering firm in Manchester and only became involved in the motor car industry later in life. He built his first car in 1904 and also met Charles Rolls that year. Rolls had studied at Cambridge University, where he had been captain of the University Bicycle Club. In 1896, at the age of 18, he travelled to France and bought his first car, a Peugeot Phaeton. This Peugeot was believed to be the first car based in Cambridge. The Rolls-Royce Company was founded in 1906.

Mark Saggers (b. 1959), the BBC and Sky Sports journalist, was born in Cambridge and attended the Perse School from 1970 to 1977. As a schoolboy he was a regular on the Newmarket Road End terrace at Cambridge United Football Club. Saggers played cricket as a specialist wicket-keeper for Cambridgeshire County Cricket Club during the 1980s, although he averaged only 3.5 runs with the bat. He also represented England at hockey.

Ronald Searle (1920–2011) was born in Newmarket Road, Cambridge, the son of a railway porter. He is best known as the inventor of the fictional girls' school St Trinian's (1948). He studied at the Cambridge School of Art (now part of the Anglia Ruskin University) and made a career in graphic art. He was captured by the Japanese in the Second World War and spent time in the infamous Changi prison camp and elsewhere. His drawings of his experiences as a prisoner of war were later published as two books, *Forty Drawings* and *To the Kwai and Back: War Drawings, 1939–1945*. After the war he worked on drawings for book and magazine illustration, theatre, film and political caricature. A frequent visitor to the Fitzwilliam Museum during his formative years, his work was presented to the museum by his children in 2014.

Clive Sinclair (b. 1940), pioneer of the pocket calculator and producer of many of the first affordable personal computers, the ZX80, ZX81 and ZX Spectrum, ran his business from Cambridgeshire. He relocated to Cambridge from London in 1967 and then had premises in St Ives. In 1982, he converted a former mineral water bottling plant in Willis Road into the company headquarters and also bought Milton Hall as a research centre. A later invention, the single-seater electric C5 car, was a failure and the business was sold off to Amstrad in 1986.

Harry Smith (1787–1860), soldier and 'Hero of Aliwal', was born in Whittlesey, the son of a surgeon. He served with distinction in the Napoleonic Wars, at Waterloo and in America, South Africa and India. He took part in the British invasion of the United States in 1812, where he witnessed the burning of Washington and the destruction of the interior of the White House. Smith was the standard bearer at the funeral of his erstwhile commander the Duke of Wellington. He and his Spanish wife Juana are both buried in Whittlesey and the Sir Harry Smith Community College is named after him. The towns of Harrismith, Smithfield and Ladysmith in South Africa are also named in the couple's honour.

Louis Smith (b. 1989), Olympic-medal-winning gymnast and *Strictly Come Dancing* champion, was born in Peterborough and attended Arthur Mellows Village College in Glinton. He trains at Huntingdon Olympic Gymnastic Club, as does Daniel Keatings, who was the first British man to win a gold medal at a major championships in 2010.

Baptist preacher **Charles Spurgeon** was baptised in the River Lark at Isleham Ferry in 1850. Later that year he moved to Cambridge and soon began his preaching career at Teversham and then Waterbeach. Soon he was addressing packed halls in London. Spurgeon drew record-breaking crowds, most notably nearly 24,000 people at the Crystal Palace in October 1857. His weekly sermons were printed and distributed as far afield as America and Australia. They were translated into nearly forty languages from Arabic to Urdu, selling over 100 million copies.

Around 60,000 people queued to view his coffin when he died in 1892.

Jane Stuart (1686–c.1773), widely acknowledged to be the natural daughter of King James II who was deposed in the 'Glorious Revolution' of 1688, lived and died in Wisbech. She was a Quaker and may have fled persecution in London. She earned a living reaping the fields and spinning wool and flax.

Mary Bates Tealby (c.1802–65), founder of the Battersea Dogs Home, was born in Huntingdon and lived there until she married.

Olympic sprinter and TV presenter **Iwan Thomas** (b.1974) lived in Godmanchester and went to Hinchingbrooke School in Huntingdon. Thomas was a member of the Great Britain 4×400 metres relay team at the 1997 World Athletics Championships in Athens, where the team came second to the USA. In 2008 one of the USA team members admitted to having taken performance-enhancing drugs and the American team was retrospectively disqualified. New gold medals were minted for the British team and Thomas received his gold at a presentation in May 2010.

Andrew Wiles (b. 1953), the man who solved Fermat's Last Theorem, was born in Cambridge. He said: 'I was a ten year old and one day I happened to be looking in my local public library and I found a book on maths and it told a bit about the history of this problem and I, a ten year old, could understand it. From that moment I tried to solve it myself, it was such a challenge, such a beautiful problem, this problem was Fermat's Last Theorem.' The problem had been unsolved for 300 years. The library was Milton Road Library in Cambridge.

Wiles went on to study for a doctorate at Clare College before becoming a professor in America. While a faculty member at Princeton University in New Jersey in the 1980s, Wiles embarked on a solitary, seven-year quest to solve the problem of Fermat's Last Theorem, working in his attic and telling no one but his wife. He went on to make an historic announcement at a conference in his home town of Cambridge, in June 1993, only to hear from a colleague two months later that his proof contained a serious mistake. But after another frantic year of work and with the help of one of his former students, Richard Taylor, he was able to re-submit the proof.

In 2016 Sir Andrew Wiles was awarded the Abel Prize, the equivalent of a Nobel Prize, the most recent of many awards to recognise his achievement.

Clive Woodward (b. 1956), the man who led the England rugby team to World Cup glory in 2003, was born in Ely, at the RAF (Princess of Wales) Hospital. His father was a pilot in the RAF.

14

ON THIS DAY

1 January 1660: The very first entry in Samuel Pepys' diary, in which he writes: 'Blessed be God, at the end of the last year I was in very good health, without any sense of my old pain'

2 January 1864: John Green is executed, the last person to be publicly executed in Cambridgeshire

3 January 1641: Jeremiah Horrocks, early astronomer and student at Emmanuel College, dies aged 22

4 January 1965: T.S. Eliot, author of the poem 'Little Gidding', dies

5 January 1962: Political journalist Andrew Rawnsley, student at Sidney Sussex College, is born

6 January 1946: Syd Barrett of Pink Floyd is born in Glisson Road, Cambridge

7 January 1536: Catherine of Aragon dies at Kimbolton Castle in Huntingdonshire. She would later be buried at Peterborough Cathedral

8 January: Feast day of St Pega, after whom the village of Peakirk is named

9 January 1995: Comedian Peter Cook, a member of the Cambridge University Footlights Club in 1960, dies aged 57

10 January 1985: The C5, a battery-powered solo car developed by Clive Sinclair in St Ives, is launched at Alexandra Palace

11 January 1941: Oakington RAF base opens

12 January 1895: The National Trust is created, co-founded by Octavia Hill of Wisbech

13 January 1644: Oliver Cromwell leaves his home in Ely for Cambridge and London

14 January 1978: Olympic athlete and former Gonville and Caius student Harold Abrahams dies

15 January 1901: The *London Gazette* reports the award of the VC to Major Alexis Doxat for service in the Boer War. Major Doxat is buried in Cambridge Cemetery

16 January 1941: King George VI visits RAF Oakington

17 January 1612: Thomas Fairfax, politician, general, and Parliamentary commander-in-chief during the English Civil War, is born. Fairfax was a student at St John's College in Cambridge during the 1620s

18 January 1941: King George VI and Queen Elizabeth visit the RAF hospital at Ely

19 January 1930: British philosopher, mathematician and economist Frank Plumpton Ramsey, a close friend of Ludwig Wittgenstein, is born in Cambridge

20 January 1651: The founder of modern comparative anatomy, Edward Tyson, is born. He earned his MD at Cambridge University in 1678

21 January 1876: The Abbots Ripton rail crash happens when a northbound London to Leeds passenger train, a southbound Edinburgh to London express and a local coal train all collide in snowy conditions. Thirteen people are killed

22 January 1788: George Gordon Byron, who famously kept a bear at Trinity College, is born

23 January 1806: William Pitt the Younger, a former student of Pembroke College, dies

24 January 1974: The *Cambridge Evening News* reports that boys will be admitted to the Cambridge Girls Grammar School for the first time. It will become Parkside Comprehensive School

25 January 2006: A visitor to the Fitzwilliam Museum in Cambridge tumbles down a staircase and breaks three valuable Chinese porcelain vases

26 January 1885: Mechanical engineer Harry Ricardo is born. He studied civil engineering at Trinity College in Cambridge before moving on to set up his own company, where he carried out much work on the development of the internal combustion engine, including the first proper tank engine in 1916

27 January 1994: The *Hunts Post* publishes a special 100th anniversary edition

28 January 1933: While a student at Cambridge University, Choudhry Rahmet Ali invents the name 'Pakistan' for a future Muslim country in southern Asia

29 January 1839: Charles Darwin marries Emma Wedgwood

30 January 1661: The body of former Lord Protector Oliver Cromwell is exhumed and his head is cut off

31 January 1892: Baptist preacher Charles Spurgeon, who began his career preaching at Teversham and Waterbeach, dies aged 57

1 February 1879: The National Skating Association is set up in Cambridge

2 February 1799: Elizabeth Woodcock, while walking from Histon to Impington, falls into a snowdrift and lies there for eight days

3 February 1970: The actor and former Yaxley resident Warwick Davis is born

4 February 1989: A deactivation ceremony at RAF Molesworth ends its association with nuclear weapons

5 February 1985: The eviction of protesters at the Molesworth Peace camp begins

6 February 1945: Two B-17 bombers crash while assembling and come down at Prickwillow and Wicken, killing two civilians

7 February 1972: Peterhouse's Olympic gold medallist Steph Cook is born

8 February 1672: Isaac Newton reads his first ever paper on optics before the Royal Society in London

9 February 1905: David Cecil, later Lord Burleigh, who famously took part in the Trinity race around the Great Court, is born at Stamford

10 February 1799: Elizabeth Woodcock is finally rescued after eight days' entombment in snow at Impington

11 February 1941: A Wellington bomber crashes in Histon Road, Cambridge, killing two elderly ladies

12 February 1322: The central Norman tower of Ely Cathedral collapses. It is later replaced by the timber Octagon

13 February 1917: The *London Gazette* reports the award of the DCM and Belgian Croix de Guerre to Joe Bailey of Soham

14 February 1951: HRH Princess Alice, Duchess of Gloucester, visits the RAF hospital in Ely

15 February 1967: The Jimi Hendrix Experience performs in Cambridge at the Dorothy Ballroom

16 February 1941: A German Junkers Ju 88A aircraft lands at Steeple Morden, believing it was in France

17 February 1890: Birth of the controversial geneticist and statistician Sir Ronald Fisher. He taught at Cambridge University from 1940 until his retirement in 1956, and became famous for disputing the evidence that smoking causes cancer

18 February 1943: First test of FIDO, the Second World War fog dispersal system, at Graveley

19 February 1943: Birth of the biochemist and molecular physiologist Tim Hunt. A graduate of Clare College in Cambridge, he shared the 2001 Nobel Prize in Physiology or Medicine for his part in discovering the protein molecules that control the cell division

20 February 1921: Burwell's war memorial is unveiled

21 February 1846: The James and Headly iron foundry on Market Hill in Cambridge burns down

22 February 1925: Death of Sir Thomas Clifford Allbutt, inventor of the clinical thermometer in Cambridge

23 February 1673: John Howland from Fenstanton, who sailed on the *Mayflower*, dies in America

24 February 1942: The steamship SS *Huntingdon* is torpedoed and sunk in the North Atlantic by a German U-boat

25 February 1601: The Earl of Essex, Chancellor of the University of Cambridge, is executed at the Tower of London for high treachery

26 February 1608: Death of John Still, Bishop of Bath and Wells 1593–1608. After graduating from Christ's College in Cambridge he rose swiftly in the University, first becoming Master of St John's College, then Master of Trinity College, and by the 1570s he had become University Vice-Chancellor

27 February 1812: The poet Lord Byron gives his first address as a member of the House of Lords, in defence of Luddite violence against industrialism. Byron was a student at Trinity College in Cambridge, engaging in sexual escapades, boxing, horse riding and gambling

28 February 1953: Crick and Watson announce they have cracked the structure of DNA at the Eagle pub in Cambridge

1 March 1986: Admission charges are first introduced at Ely Cathedral

2 March 1817: The Rockingham Coach is overturned by high wind on the North Road near Kate's Cabin in Hunts, injuring several passengers

3 March 1920: Artist Ronald Searle is born in Cambridge

4 March 1943: A Lancaster bomber crashes just outside Yaxley. Pilot Officer Kujundzic stayed at the controls to avoid hitting the village

5 March 1252: Henry III's charter grants the tolls on the St Ives Fair to Huntingdon Borough

6 March 1946: David Gilmour of Pink Floyd is born in Cambridge

7 March 1615: James I visits Cambridge

8 March 1838: The Coronation Feast takes place on Parker's Piece in Cambridge, with a hot air balloon flight, too

9 March 1792: The senate of Cambridge University votes to petition the House of Commons for the abolition of the slave trade

10 March 1946: Eileen Lenton becomes the first woman police officer appointed in Huntingdonshire

11 March 1961: The first families from London move into the Oxmoor housing estate, Huntingdon

12 March 1864: The neurologist William H.R. Rivers is born. He became a fellow of St John's College in Cambridge and was best known for his work treating First World War officers who were suffering from shell shock

13 March 1764: Prime Minister and former Trinity College student Earl Grey is born

14 March 2015: The Tivoli pub in Cambridge is destroyed by fire

15 March 1779: Queen Victoria's first Prime Minister and former Trinity student Lord Melbourne is born

16 March 1973: Pink Floyd's album *The Dark Side of the Moon* is released

17 March 1780: Elizabeth Butchill is executed at the County Gaol for the murder of her bastard child by throwing her into the river

18 March 1745: The first British Prime Minister and former King's College student Robert Walpole dies

19 March 1963: The Beatles play at the Regal in Cambridge

20 March 1908: The actor Michael Redgrave is born. He was a student at Magdalene College in Cambridge before moving on to acting; he starred in many notable films of the 1940s and '50s, including *Dead of Night* and *The Dambusters*

21 March 1918: Fifteen Huntingdonshire soldiers die on this day in the last year of the First World War

22 March 1785: The geologist Adam Sedgwick is born. After his death in Cambridge in 1873 it was proposed that the University's geology museum should be enlarged in his honour; it was renamed the Sedgwick Museum in 1903

23 March 1918: Lt Wastell is killed when his aircraft crashes into the spire of St Ives church

24 March 1747: John Bigg of Grafham bequeaths £150 to the poor of Grafham parish

25 March 1960: Cromwell's head is buried in a secret location within the chapel of Sidney Sussex College

26 March 1983: Anthony Blunt, revealed to be one of the Cambridge Spies, dies

27 March 1969: The official opening of Oakdale Primary School in Stanground

28 March 1760: Anti-slavery campaigner Thomas Clarkson is born in Wisbech

29 March 1943: Huntingdon MP and British Prime Minister John Major is born in Surrey

30 March 2002: Queen Elizabeth, the first woman to receive a degree from Cambridge University, dies aged 101

31 March 1654: The Bedford Level Company commissions Jonas Moore to create 'one general complete map of the whole level of the Fens'. Moore's map of the Great Level was first published four years later

1 April 1965: Mid Anglia Constabulary is formed by the amalgamation of the Cambridge Borough, Cambridge County, Peterborough, Isle of Ely and Huntingdonshire forces

2 April 2012: RAF Brampton loses its status as an RAF Base

3 April 1802: William Wright of Foxton and John Bullock of Bedfordshire are executed at Cambridge Castle for forging banknotes

4 April 1789: Francis and Thomas Brown are hanged at the County Gaol for burglary in Castle Camps

5 April 1923: George Herbert, the 5th Earl of Carnarvon and a former Trinity College Cambridge student, dies in Egypt after accidentally shaving an infected mosquito bite. His death was popularly attributed to Tutankhamun's 'curse'

6 April 1857: Huntingdonshire Constabulary is formed

7 April 1779: Martha Ray, the long-time mistress of the Earl of Sandwich, of Hinchingbrooke House in Huntingdon, is shot dead on the steps of the Royal Opera House

8 April 1904: The economist John Hicks is born. He lectured in economics at Cambridge during the 1930s and later in life he was awarded the Nobel Prize for Economics for his work on welfare theory

9 April 1910: The first flight by a Bleriot monoplane from Portholme Meadow in Huntingdon

10 April 1778: The social commentator, critic, painter and essayist William Hazlitt is born. His parents had met and married in Wisbech. During the 1760s his father, William Hazlitt senior, was a Unitarian pastor in Wisbech when he met Grace Loftus, an ironmonger's daughter

11 April 1953: Andrew Wiles, who solved Fermat's Last Theorem, is born in Cambridge

12 April 1639: The English naturalist and physician Martin Lister is born. He later became a fellow of St John's College in Cambridge and was the first person to carry out a scientific study of spiders

13 April 1850: Mary Reader and Elias Lucas are hanged at Cambridge for poisoning Susan Lucas

14 April 1872: The British–Indian scholar Abdullah Yusuf Ali is born in Bombay. He studied at St John's College in Cambridge and his famous translation into English of the Koran, first published in the 1930s, is still widely read today

15 April 1875: A coin hoard is discovered in the old Hall at Pembroke College

16 April 1705: Queen Anne knights Isaac Newton in Cambridge

17 April 1957: The novelist Nick Hornby is born. A student of Jesus College in Cambridge, his books include *Fever Pitch*, *High Fidelity* and *About a Boy*

18 April 1953: Opening ceremony of Waterbeach School

19 April 1882: Naturalist Charles Darwin dies

20 April 1737: Cambridge town sessions demand that 'Mad Tom', who had been walking the streets of Cambridge armed with a sword and other weapons, be arrested

21 April 1946: John Maynard Keynes, economist and former High Steward of Cambridge, dies

22 April 1989: Gymnast Louis Smith is born in Peterborough

23 April 1989: The actor Nigel Hawthorne opens Hinchingbrooke Country Park in Huntingdon

24 April 1731: Daniel Defoe dies in London. During the 1720s Defoe visited Cambridgeshire as part of *A Tour thro' the Thole Island of Great Britain*, seeing Stourbridge Fair in particular

25 April 1599: Oliver Cromwell is born in Huntingdonshire

26 April 1915: William Rhodes Moorhouse is fatally injured in an air mission. He is later awarded a VC for his bravery

27 April 1603: James I stays at Hinchingbroke House in Huntingdon

28 April 1789: Fletcher Christian leads a mutiny against Captain William Bligh on board HMS *Bounty*. Both Fletcher and Bligh had earlier served on the 80-gun warship HMS *Cambridge*

29 April 1951: Philosopher Ludwig Wittgenstein dies in Cambridge. He is buried a few days later in the Parish of the Ascension Burial Ground on Huntingdon Road

30 April 1914: King George V has Suffragette leaflets thrown at his car in Cambridge

1 May 1982: Radio Cambridgeshire goes on air for the first time

2 May 1646: King Charles I pays a visit to the Ferrar community at Little Gidding

3 May 1977: A Canberra bomber from RAF Wyton crashes onto houses in the Oxmoor estate, Huntingdon, killing five people

4 May 1924: Cambridge University Catholic Chaplaincy, Fisher House, is officially opened

5 May 1818: Karl Marx is born in Prussia. Marx wrote about the appalling living conditions of workers in various Cambridgeshire and Huntingdonshire villages, including Gamlingay and Hartford, in volume one of *Das Kapital*

6 May 1789: A prize fight is held at Stilton between a Huntingdon local called Humphries and a Jewish fighter called Mendoza. The bout was watched by 3,000 spectators and was in the end won by Mendoza. The fight was swiftly moved elsewhere because Stilton constables arrived halfway through to break it up

7 May 1840: The inaugural meeting of the Cambridge Antiquarian Society is held at St John's College

8 May 2007: A concert to celebrate the 800th anniversary of the Mayoralty in Cambridge is held at the Guild Hall

9 May 1941: Hundreds of incendiary bombs fall in the area between Hills Road and Trumpington Road in Cambridge. Fifty houses received direct hits, yet all but four or five of the resulting fires were put out within minutes

10 May 1945: Crews from RAF Witchford are involved in Operation *Exodus*, repatriating thousands of Allied prisoners of war from Germany

11 May 1812: Prime Minister Spencer Percival is shot by John Bellingham from St Neots

12 May 1937: There are celebrations in towns and villages throughout the county to mark the coronation of King George VI and Queen Elizabeth

13 May 1615: James I visits Cambridge

14 May 1912: Demonstration of a new fire engine in Ely, where firemen hose down the Corn Exchange

15 May 1953: Official opening of St Audrey's School, Ely

16 May 1984: Official opening, by the Queen, of the Grafton Centre shopping precinct in Cambridge

17 May 1938: RAF Alconbury opens as a satellite base to RAF Upwood

18 May 1921: Crown Prince Hirohito, Emperor of Japan from 1926, visits Cambridge

19 May 1969: Canberra bombers leave RAF Bassingbourn for the last time, heading for Cottesmore

20 May 1942: The first American airmen arrive at Kimbolton airfield

21 May 1950: A double-decker bus is blown over by a tornado at Sutton

22 May 1816: The Littleport Riots begin when a stone is thrown through a shop window

23 May 2014: The 'Light' cinema opens to the public in Wisbech

24 May 2016: Andrew Wiles is awarded the Abel Prize for solving Fermat's Last Theorem

25 May 1936: T.S. Eliot visits Little Gidding church

26 May 1812: The exiled French King Louis XVIII visits Cambridge

27 May 1964: The first Prime Minister of an independent India and former student of Trinity College, Jawaharlal Nehru, dies

28 May 1959: Sports reporter Mark Saggers is born in Cambridge

29 May 1716: A Jacobite disturbance breaks out in Cambridge, and a meeting house is almost demolished

30 May 1938: Commemoration of fifty years of the *Cambridge Daily News*

31 May 1881: Ely Theological College is opened

1 June 1999: Inventor of the hovercraft Sir Christopher Cockerill dies

2 June 1944: 5 tons of high explosive blow up on a train at Soham railway station

3 June 1947: King George VI, a former student, returns to Trinity College for the 40th anniversary celebrations

4 June 1645: Oliver Cromwell returns to his home town of Huntingdon for the last time

5 June 1940: The first Second World War air raid in Cambridgeshire; bombs fall near Peterborough and an incendiary device goes off near Duxford

6 June 1898: Walter Horsford, the 'St Neots poisoner,' is found guilty of the murder of Annie Holmes

7 June 1958: Cambridge University students place an Austin Seven car on the roof of Senate House

8 June 1647: Charles I is held in custody at Childerley Hall

9 June 1937: The exiled Emperor Haile Selassie visits Cambridge after his country has been invaded by Italy

10 June 1905: Three people are drowned when the Fen Ditton ferry capsizes

11 June 1959: Sir Christopher Cockerill's first hovercraft, SR.N1, makes its first ever flight

12 June 1819: The Revd Charles Kingsley, social reformer and writer, is born. A graduate of Magdalene College in Cambridge, he went on to write the novel *Westward Ho!*, which led to a village being named after it

13 June 1667: Samuel Pepys sends his wife to bury gold coins in his garden in Brampton for safekeeping

14 June 1910: James Hancock is the last person to suffer the death penalty in Cambridgeshire

15 June 1911: Wilbert Vere Awdry is born in Hampshire. Better known as the Reverend W. Awdry, he would later become Rector of Elsworth with Knapwell in Cambridgeshire and write the Thomas the Tank Engine books

16 June 1978: The movie *Grease* starring Cambridge-born singer Olivia Newton-John is released

17 June 1939: Centenary celebration of Bourn Methodist Church

18 June 1940: Eleven people are killed when bombs fell on Vicarage Terrace in Cambridge, the first British civilian casualties of the war

19 June 1917: The City of Ely War Shrine is unveiled

20 June 1844: Frederick Augustus, King of Saxony, visits Cambridge

21 June 1887: A dinner to celebrate the Golden Jubilee of Queen Victoria is held in the Market Place, Wisbech

22 June 1856: The writer Sir Henry Rider Haggard, author of *King Solomon's Mines* and *She*, is born. In 1901 Rider Haggard journeyed through Cambridgeshire and Huntingdonshire to gather material on living conditions for his book *Rural England*

23 June 1827: An Act for building a new town prison for Cambridge is passed

24 June 1741: A daily postal service is established between Cambridge and London

25 June 1772: John Bardolph's will of this date bequeaths money to the parish of St Mary's church in Huntingdon to purchase annually new coats and new pairs of shoes for four poor Huntingdon men

26 June 1973: Severe damage is caused to buildings and trees by a tornado passing over Parson's Drove and Tydd St Giles

27 June 1970: Campkin Road, Cambridge, is flooded by heavy rainfall

28 June 1816: The Littleport Rioters are executed

29 June 1953: Dedication of the new Downham College chapel

30 June 1906: A great fire breaks out at Fyfe's forage factory in Littleport

1 July 1916: The first day of the Somme: Buckden-born John Leslie Green of the Royal Army Medical Corps is killed, and is later awarded the VC

2 July 2013: Alan Titchmarsh's *Love Your Garden* programme features the Sola family from Cambridgeshire

3 July 1799: Elizabeth Woodcock, who fell into a snowdrift while walking from Histon to Impington, dies, possibly from all the alcohol she had been given to celebrate her escape

4 July 1948: Some 900 women who had been denied degrees by the University are honoured in Senate House

5 July 1945: Arthur Symonds is elected as the first Labour MP for Cambridge in the Labour landslide at the 1945 general election, winning by a majority of only 682 votes over the incumbent Conservative MP Richard Tufnell

6 July 1553: Mary Tudor flees to Sawston Hall when her brother Edward VI dies

7 July 2006: Pink Floyd's 'Syd' Barrett dies

8 July 1607: St Mary's church in Huntingdon collapses

9 July 1889: The River Cam Bridges Act is published to allow the construction of the Victoria Avenue bridge and Abbey Road bridges

10 July 1648: The Battle of St Neots. A small force of Roundheads defeat a force of 300 Cavaliers

11 July 1931: The Ortona Bus Company of Cambridge is taken over by the Eastern Counties Omnibus Company, based in Norwich. The Green Ortona buses change to the red of Eastern Counties

12 July 1814: The Cambridge Peace Festival dinner for 6,000 people is held on Parker's Piece

13 July 1967: Burwell Village College is opened

14 July 1935: Cambridge Royal Mail sorting office opens

15 July 1630: A new charter from Charles I changes the constitution of the borough of Huntingdon, and upsets Oliver Cromwell so much that he moves to St Ives

16 July 1931: Emperor Haile Selassie, an Honorary Doctor of Law from Cambridge University, signs the first constitution of Ethiopia

17 July 1924: Tefari Makonnen, later the Emperor Haile Selasse, receives an Honourary Doctorate at Cambridge

18 July 1766: Cambridge town sessions demand that a ducking chair be placed at Magdalene Bridge to punish scolds and disorderly women

19 July 1920: A 'Pedlar from Paris' arrives in St John's Street Cambridge to sell French hats, dresses and lingerie

20 July 1793: The *Cambridge Intelligencer* newspaper is launched by Benjamin Flow

21 July 1964: The official opening of March Fire Station

22 July 1892: The cricketer Jack MacBryan is born. He studied at Jesus College and played for the Cambridge University cricket team. He played in his only Test Match in 1925, which was ruined by rain, and he remains the only Test cricketer who neither batted, bowled nor dismissed anyone in the field. *Wisden* named him as one of their cricketers of the year in 1925

23 July 1705: Birth of the antiquary Francis Blomefield. As a boy he enjoyed recording monumental inscriptions from churches he visited in Norfolk, Suffolk and Cambridgeshire, and in 1751 published his Cambridgeshire notes as a single volume entitled *Collectanea Cantabrigiensia*. He died of smallpox the following year

24 July 1921: Dedication of the Wisbech war memorial

25 July 1957: The Mullard Radio Astronomy Observatory is opened at Barton Road in Cambridge

26 July 1774: Lord Orford is hit by a storm whilst sailing in Whittlesey Mere

27 July 1625: Edward Montagu of Hinchingbrooke, 1st Earl of Sandwich, Civil War General, Admiral and patron of Samuel Pepys is born

28 July 1942: Bombs fall on Bridge Street and Sidney Street and incendiaries cause a fire at the Union Society building in Cambridge. Three people are killed, ten buildings are destroyed and 127 others damaged

29 July 1833: Thomas Clarkson's fellow anti-slavery campaigner and former St John's College student William Wilberforce dies

30 July 1785: John Peters is executed at the County Gaol for stealing a silver spoon in Barnwell, Cambridge

31 July 1957: HRH Princess Margaret lays the foundation stone for the Good Shepherd Church in Arbury, Cambridge

1 August 1907: James Berry Walford founds the Ortona Motor Bus Co. in Cambridge

2 August 1945: The Freedom of the Borough of Cambridge is conferred on the US Army Air Force, which had operated from bases around Cambridge

3 August 1916: King George V visits the First Eastern General Hospital in Cambridge

4 August 1938: The first operational Spitfire arrives at Duxford airfield

5 August 1914: The Cambridgeshire Regiment is mobilised and forms up in Cambridge

6 August 1963: Cherry Hinton Branch Library opens

7 August 2011: The St Ives to Cambridge Guided Busway opens

8 August 1643: Oliver Cromwell visits Peterborough

9 August 1564: Queen Elizabeth I progresses around various colleges as part of her visit to Cambridge

10 August 1871: Emperor Pedro of Brazil visits Cambridge

11 August 1850: The Great Northern Railway opens its new railway station at Huntingdon

12 August 1266: The Jews of Cambridge are attacked and robbed by the 'disinherited' Barons of the Isle of Ely. Many were slaughtered

13 August 1974: Snooker player Joe Perry is born in Wisbech

14 August 1984: Former Trinity Hall student J.B. Priestley dies aged 89

15 August 1941: Josef Jakobs, a German spy captured in Ramsey, is executed at the Tower of London

16 August 1703: Cambridge Corporation demands that the pesthouses on Coldham's Common be demolished

17 August 1847: The St Ives to Cambridge railway is opened to traffic

18 August 1944: Glenn Miller and his band perform at Steeple Morden Airfield

19 August 1718: Mary Bragg bequeaths 10 shillings to be distributed annually among the poor of Hemingford Grey parish, 'having first regards to the poor old maids'

20 August 1944: Trinity student Rajiv Ghandi is born

21 August 1928: Athlete and St John's College student Chris Brasher is born

22 August 1942: The Luftwaffe bomb Ramsey with at least five high-explosive devices, killing seven and injuring many more

23 August 1945: Queen Mary is seen in Cambridge shopping at Mr Stanley Woolston's antique shop.

24 August 1645: Royalist and Parliamentarian forces fight the Battle of Huntingdon

25 August 1876: Social reformer and founder of the Save the Children organisation Eglantyne Jebb is born

26 August: Feast day of St Pandionia, who is buried in the church that bears her name at Eltisley

27 August 1921: The Central Cinema opens in Hobson Street, Cambridge

28 August 1976: An American C-141 Starlifter cargo plane crashes during a thunderstorm at Thorney Toll, killing all eighteen on board

29 August 1977: The national parascending championships are held at Oakington

30 August 1768: King Christian VII of Denmark and Norway visits Cambridge

31 August 1963: Spicer's cinema in Sawston closes

1 September 1939: Evacuees from London start arriving in the county

2 September 1914: A Red Cross Hospital opens in Huntingdon

3 September 1939: A Blenheim bomber from RAF Wyton carries out the RAF's very first operation of the Second World War, when it takes off to photograph the German navy.

4 September 1541: Peterborough Abbey becomes a cathedral

5 September 1976: A military flying spectacular is held to celebrate Burma Star Day at Waterbeach Barracks

6 September 1594: A great flood, caused by heavy rainfall, sweeps away Cambridge's Great Bridge and two further bridges at King's College and St John's College

7 September: The first day of Stourbridge Fair during the seventeenth and eighteenth centuries

8 September 1727: The Burwell fire kills seventy-eight people

9 September 1994: A report on the escape of six prisoners from Whitemoor Prison is released

10 September 1914: A request is made to form a Cambridgeshire Volunteer Battalion

11 September 1994: A memorial at the former RAF base at Castle Camps is unveiled

12 September 1905: Opening ceremony of Haddenham Baptist Chapel

13 September 1894: Trinity Hall student and author J.B. Priestley is born

14 September 1864: A huge fire at Chatteris destroys more than 100 houses

15 September 1849: Eight houses are destroyed in the 'Great Fire' of Cambridge

16 September 1912: Army Airship *Beta II* lands at Jesus Grove

17 September 1912: Army Airship *Gamma II* lands at Kneesworth

18 September 1967: Sir John Cockcroft, director of Britain's Atomic Energy Research Establishment during the 1940s and '50s and the first Master of Churchill College, dies in Cambridge. He is buried a few days later in the parish of the Ascension burial ground on Huntingdon Road

19 September 1938: Official opening of the Whittlesey Sewage Works

20 September 1889: The first parachute descent in Cambridgeshire probably took place on this date

21 September 1944: Bing Crosby visits USAAF airfields in Huntingdonshire to boost war morale for American service personnel

22 September 1744: The first Cambridge newspaper, the *Cambridge Journal and Weekly Flying Post*, is published. It was started by Robert Walker and Thomas James and printed 'next to the Theatre Coffee House'

23 September 1917: Norris Knight crashes his aircraft into a garden in Barnes Walk, St Ives

24 September 1971: The opening of Huntingdon's first purpose-built library. It would be demolished and replaced by a new one in 2009

25 September 1921: Sutton railway station is gutted by fire

26 September 1948: Olivia Newton John is born in Cambridge

27 September 1681: Charles II and Queen Catherine of Braganza visit Cambridge

28 September 1680: Mary of Modena, wife of James II, with the future Queens Mary and Anne visit Cambridge

29 September 1982: Amy Williams, British skeleton racer and an Olympic gold medallist, is born in Cambridge

30 September 1975: County Surveyor Richard Dorling opens the Huntingdon bypass, now part of the A14

1 October 1899: William Beattie opens a hairdresser's shop in Jesus Lane; he celebrates his 50th anniversary at the same premises in 1949

2 October 1910: A.L. Symmonds, Cambridge's first Labour MP, is born in Cambridge

3 October 1799: Cambridge celebrates Nelson's victory at the Battle of the Nile with illuminations, a parade, a public supper, and a collection of money to support the widows and orphans of the battle

4 October 1671: Charles II visits Cambridge

5 October 1942: A Wellington bomber crashes onto cottages in Somersham, killing eleven people

6 October 1892: Trinity College student Alfred Lord Tennyson dies

7 October 1689: King William III visits the Wren Library

8 October 1983: The largest bomber in the world, the American B-52, lands at Duxford to go on display at the Imperial War Museum

9 October 1918: Queen Mary visits the Papworth Tuberculosis Colony

10 October 2000: Anglian Water workmen discover the Magdalene Coin Hoard

11 October 1677: Cornelius Vermuyden, lead engineer of the project to drain the Cambridgeshire Fens, dies in London

12 October 1216: King John loses the Crown Jewels near Wisbech

13 October 1766: Addenbrookes Hospital opens in Trumpington Street

14 October 1916: The Cambridgeshire Regiment attacks and holds the Schwaben Redoubt during the Battle of the Somme

15 October 1363: A Charter granted by Edward III reports that Huntingdon is desolate and ruined after the Black Death

16 October 1555: The 'Ely Martyrs' William Wolsey and Robert Pygot are burnt at the stake in Ely for heresy

17 October: Feast day of St Etheldreda, patron saint of Cambridge and the founder of the convent at Ely

18 October 1917: The *London Gazette* announces the award of the Military Medal to Albert Hurl of St Ives for gallantry in the Machine Gun Corps

19 October 1446: Death of Sir William Allington of Horseheath, speaker of the House of Commons

20 October 1955: Queen Elizabeth II opens the School of Veterinary Medicine in Madingley Road, Cambridge

21 October 1948: Queen Elizabeth becomes the first woman to receive a degree from Cambridge University

22 October 1934: The new University Library building is opened by King George V

23 October 1901: The Oliver Cromwell statue in St Ives is unveiled

24 October 1940: An example of Germany's most modern bomber, a Dornier Do 215, is shot down over St Neots

25 October 1800: Thomas Babington Macaulay, essayist and politician, is born. He studied at Trinity College and is best known for his five-volume *History of England*

26 October 1843: Queen Victoria and Prince Albert visit Cambridge

27 October 1833: Priscilla Peckover, founder of the Peace Union, is born in Wisbech

28 October 1976: Princess Margaret visits Cambridge

29 October 1988: Steve Cram and Sebastian Coe attempt the Trinity Great Court Run

30 October 1762: The *Cambridge Chronicle* is first published, priced at 2½d weekly and aimed at a University audience

31 October 1789: A handbill is issued offering a £100 reward for the return of items stolen from Trinity College

1 November 1643: The clergyman, historian and biographer John Strype is born. After graduating from Catharine Hall in the University of Cambridge he went on to write numerous biographies of leading Reformation-era Protestants

2 November 1917: The *Cambs Times* reports that A.H. Ruston of St Ives, a Lieutenant Commander in the Armoured Car Squadron, has been awarded the Order of Vladimir

3 November 1913: Frederick Seekings is hanged, the last man to be executed in Cambridgeshire

4 November 1958: The official opening of Swavesey Village College

5 November 1929: The airship R101 flies over Cambridge on its way to Sandringham. The R101 would later crash in France in 1930

6 November 1943: Two Wellington bombers collide over Huntingdon

7 November 1848: Mill Road Cemetery in Cambridge is consecrated by the Bishop of Ely

8 November 1674: John Milton, poet and former student at Christ's College, dies

9 November 1977: Formal opening of Wolfson College, Cambridge by the Queen

10 November 1944: A V2 rocket lands near Fulbourn

11 November 1918: Armistice celebrations are held across the county

12 November 1842: Birth of the scientist John William Strutt, 3rd Baron Rayleigh. He became the second Cavendish Professor of Physics at the University of Cambridge. He discovered argon (for which he was awarded the 1904 Nobel Prize for Physics) but perhaps more interestingly he discovered the phenomenon now called 'Rayleigh scattering', which explains why the sky appears blue and the sun appears yellow

13 November 1820: The 'Battle of Peas Hill', Cambridge, a reaction to the acquittal of Queen Caroline

14 November 1989: The Royal Mail issues Christmas stamps featuring Ely Cathedral

15 November 1961: 'The Adoration of the Magi' by Rubens is acquired by King's College in Cambridge. They would later install it at the east end of the chapel, generating much controversy

16 November 1979: Anthony Blunt is revealed as the fourth of the Cambridge Spies

17 November 1834: Mr Mite of Godmanchester dies aged 90. It was written of him that 'he is said to have always expressed a hope that he should not be a day ill before his death, and this desire was singularly fulfilled, for he died after a few hours confinement to his bed'

18 November 2012: Death of Sir Philip Ledger, director of music at King's College in Cambridge from 1974 to 1982.

He directed the famous Festival of Nine Lessons and Carols on many occasions and took the King's College Choir on their first ever tour of the USA

19 November 2009: Queen Elizabeth II visits Ely

20 November 1851: Captain George Davies of the Royal Navy is appointed Chief Constable of Cambridgeshire's first countywide police force

21 November 1785: Messrs Poole and Armstrong ascend in a hot air balloon from Trinity Hall Close in Cambridge

22 November 1783: A Mr Astley carries out the first balloon flight over Cambridge

23 November 1973: Queen Elizabeth II visits Ely

24 November 1956: The Tivoli and Playhouse Cinemas in Cambridge are closed down

25 November 2000: Anthony Russell, the 68th Bishop of Ely, is enthroned at Ely Cathedral

26 November 1670: Prince William of Orange, the future King William III, visits Cambridge

27 November 1990: Huntingdon MP John Major is declared leader of the Conservative Party, and therefore Prime Minster as well, following the fall of Margaret Thatcher

28 November 1935: The St Neots Quads are born

29 November 1917: George Clare is killed at the Battle of Cambrai. He is later posthumously awarded the VC

30 November 1979: Pink Floyd's album *The Wall* is released

1 December 1961: The opening ceremony of Burwell School

2 December 1943: The *Hunts Post* reports on an explosion at RAF Wyton that killed two passers-by and demolished seven cottages

3 December 1944: The Home Guard in Cambridgeshire is officially stood down

4 December 1983: An arson attack occurs at the Victoria Cinema in Cambridge Market Square

5 December 2015: The Winter Fair is held in Mill Road, Cambridge

6 December 1991: The 'Grand Opening Day' at Fawcett Primary School

7 December 1833: John Stallan of Great Shelford is executed for arson at Cambridge

8 December 1872: Hannah Tapfield King, who was born in Cambridge, marries Brigham Young in Utah

9 December 1941: The Duke of Kent visits the RAF hospital in Ely

10 December 1892: Lucy Boston, author of the *Children of Green Knowe* stories and resident of Hemingford Grey in Huntingdonshire, is born in Lancashire. Her first Green Knowe book was published in 1954

11 December 1921: Trumpington's war memorial is dedicated and unveiled

12 December 1943: A carol festival is held at Wisbech Empire Theatre

13 December 1908: The scientist Elizabeth Alexander is born. After earning her PhD from Newnham College in Cambridge she went to Singapore to work on radar, but was safely evacuated to New Zealand before the fall of the city. After the war she became one of the first women to work in the new field of radio-astronomy

14 December 1882: Neil Primrose, Wisbech MP 1910–17, is born in Scotland

15 December 1847: Seven prisoners break out of Huntingdon Gaol

16 December 1882: England cricketer Sir Jack Hobbs is born in Cambridge

17 December 1979: England Cricket Captain Charlotte Edwards is born in Pidley

18 December 2014: Cambridge author Fred Unwin dies

19 December 1546: Henry VIII founds Trinity College in Cambridge

20 December 1643: Iconoclast William Dowsing destroys Catholic imagery in Peterhouse College Chapel, the first such incident on his tour across Cambridgeshire. 'We pulled down two mighty great angels, with wings, and diverse other angels, and the four evangelists, and Peter with his keys on the chapel door, and about a hundred cherubims and angels, and diverse superstitious letters in gold'

21 December 1505: Birth of Thomas Wriothesley, 1st Earl of Southampton. After graduating from Trinity Hall in Cambridge he became a ruthless courtier to Henry VIII, personally torturing the writer Anne Askew in the Tower of London

22 December 1884: A sermon is preached at Peterhouse to celebrate the 600th anniversary of its foundation

23 December 1855: Alan Gray, British organist and composer, is born. He attended Trinity College, Cambridge. In 1893 he returned to Cambridge to be organist at Trinity College, where he remained until 1930. He died in Cambridge, aged 79

24 December 1954: The BBC first broadcasts *The Festival of Nine Lessons and Carols*, sung by the Choir of King's College, Cambridge

25 December 1642: Astronomer and physicist Isaac Newton is born in Lincolnshire. At the age of 19 he was admitted to Trinity College in Cambridge as a student and in 1667 he was elected a Fellow there. It was while at Trinity College that Newton carried out his experiments into light using prisms

26 December 1643: The Puritan iconoclast William Dowsing visits King's College Chapel and orders the destruction of the stained-glass windows, the dismantling of the organ and the removal of 'superstitious pictures'

27 December 1831: Former Cambridge University student Charles Darwin sets sail on HMS *Beagle*

28 December 1859: Death of the politician and writer Thomas Babington Macaulay, aged 59. A graduate of Trinity College in Cambridge, he is most remembered for writing *The Lays of Ancient Rome* and *The History of England*

29 December 1916: The *Hunts Post* reports that Sergeant J.E. Denton of St Ives has been awarded the Military Medal for conspicuous bravery in the field

30 December 2011: Cambridge artist Ronald Searle dies

31 December 1818: Weston Hatfield issues the first edition of the *Cambridge and Hertford Independent Press*

ACKNOWLEDGEMENTS

First and foremost, we thank our families for all the support they have given us while we researched and wrote this book, in particular Lesley Akeroyd and Nick Clifford, and special thanks to Nick for providing some of the images and for checking the manuscript. We also thank Chris Jakes, former Cambridgeshire Local Studies Librarian, for his suggestions while we were writing this book.

This does not pretend to be a complete history of Cambridgeshire, just a taster. If you want to know more, you should visit either the Cambridgeshire Collection at Cambridge Central Library or Cambridgeshire Archives, both treasure houses of information – this is where we did our research and where many of our illustrations come from, and we are very grateful to Cambridgeshire County Council for permission to do so, especially Head of Cultural and Community Services Christine May. The Cambridgeshire Collection focusses on photographs, prints and published items, while Cambridgeshire Archives holds original documents and manuscripts. You can find out more by visiting the Cambridgeshire County Council website at www.cambridgeshire.gov.uk. For historical sources relating to Peterborough you should visit Peterborough Central Library, which has its own local studies and archive collections; https://vivacity.org/library-archives.